"This book weaves together the fascinating upbringing and unique experience of Robin John, with scriptural examples and theology. Robin shows how to express our faith, values, and passion through our work and investments, and rightly concludes that we can earn good profit while positively impacting the world. I am thankful for Robin's book, work, and friendship." —Bob Doll, CEO/CIO or Crossmark Global Investments, former chief equity strategist at BlackRock, and chief investment officer at Merrill Lynch Investment Managers

"Robin John's book *The Good Investor* is a life story with great passion that is so current in today's crazy culture. It is an excellent collaboration of scripture with handling money but in a way that comes alive to readers beyond just tithing. It is a story of adventure and dedication in a search for one's true purpose. *The Good Investor* invites the reader to believe bigger and partner with God in aligning their life, work, and wealth." —Del Harris, former NBA Coach of the Year while serving as head coach of the Los Angeles Lakers

"I highly recommend this insightful book that challenges readers to reconsider the way they approach their financial investing decisions. The book draws on Biblical principles to inspire readers to not only avoid companies that profit from ill-gotten gain but embrace businesses that practice solid stewardship—protecting the vulnerable, loving their neighbors, and serving the real needs of the world." —David Green, CEO and founder of Hobby Lobby*

"*The Good Investor* shares Robin John's compelling personal story—growing up in rural India and going on to co-found an investment firm that manages billions of dollars in assets—and offers a profound call to radically rethink the way we invest. He invites us to align faith with action, heart with head, and belief with practice to invest in ways that bring joy to the world. The book challenged my thinking, stretched my imagination, and made me reconsider the purpose and power of my financial decisions. If you want a sound investment philosophy infused with faith and purpose, this book is a must-read." —Peter Greer, president and CEO of Hope International and author of *Mission Drift* and *Lead with Prayer*

"*The Good Investor* is a call to all people looking to pursue purpose through their investments, work, and lives, to dream bigger and to be on mission with God. Robin John details his own exciting and encouraging story of coming out of poverty to go on to found a company that invests billions of dollars in line with a biblical framework. Robin shows that when the everyday person discovers their calling, they can do powerful things for the Kingdom." —Rob West, CEO of Kingdom Advisors and host of Faith & Finance Live on Moody Radio

"Years ago, Robin John asked me a powerful question that has forever changed my perspective on investing: 'If you believe all the money you have is ultimately God's, is He pleased with the way you are investing His money?' *The Good Investor* unpacks some of Robin's sound wisdom on this topic and my hope is millions read this book and consider the exponential power of capital to make the world rejoice!" —Casey Crawford, cofounder and CEO of Movement Mortgage and former NFL tight end for the Carolina Panthers and Tampa Bay Buccaneers

"Robin's authenticity and intentionality in sharing his journey and challenging investing norms illuminates the need for all of us to make the maximum positive impact on each other and on the world around us. He reminds us that we have the power to be the difference, and that by connecting faith, values, and passion with investment decisions, we can all contribute to a better world. *The Good Investor* is relatable, uplifting, and awakens readers to the avenues and opportunities for a more positive future for generations to come." —Dennis Mathew, chairman and CEO of Altice USA*

"Robin John's life story of an economically impoverished childhood and his subsequent journey in becoming a faith-based investment entrepreneur is truly inspiring. Pouring from every page of this groundbreaking book is a contagious joy, a passionate commitment, and a compelling logic to invest your financial resources to make a better world. Your eyes will be opened, your heart will be touched and your imagination stirred on how you can experience the joy of making a difference in bringing greater healing to the world. I simply cannot recommend this beautiful and brilliant book highly enough!" —Tom Nelson, founder and president of Made to Flourish and senior pastor of Christ Community Church in Kansas City

"*The Good Investor* is exceptional. This book shows you what it looks like practically to join Christ's work of redemption in the job you already have. That idea can often feel lofty, academic, and unattainable. Robin makes it supremely accessible and practical. This book will baptize your imagination in ways you didn't even know you needed—and your work will never be the same because of it." —Jordan Raynor, bestselling author of *The Sacredness of Secular Work* and *Redeeming Your Time*

"Robin John's inspiring personal story illustrates the power and potential of economic uplift. His vision for Eventide's values-based investing shows how our work can benefit everyone and not just bolster the bottom line for a fortunate few. Our world can be a much better place if investors—and employees of all kinds—will learn from his example and prioritize what really matters now, and in eternity." —Collin Hansen, vice president for Content, editor in chief of The Gospel Coalition, executive director of The Keller Center for Cultural Apologetics, and host of the Gospelbound podcast

"*The Good Investor* by Robin John invites readers into his personal journey and shares the inspiration behind the Eventide investment model that aligns with the Great Commission while delivering strong business results. Whether you're an investor or a business leader, this book will challenge your perspectives on personal and organizational investments. It offers a fresh approach to investing that prioritizes justice and doing good, providing evidence that making the world a better place can lead to profitable business practices. *The Good Investor* is a must-read for anyone curious about the intersection of faith and finance. If you've ever doubted the fruitfulness of ethical investing, this book will inspire and convince you otherwise." —Dr. Hannah Stolze, William E. Crenshaw Endowed Chair in Supply Chain Management in the Department of Management in Baylor University's Hankamer School of Business

"We need a re-envisioning of responsible investing. If all people were to follow Robin John's advice, oriented towards true flourishing, we would live in a very different, and much better, world."
—Tyler J. VanderWeele, director of the Human Flourishing Program at Harvard University

"Of the 162 million individual investors in the United States, very few of us think critically and biblically about the ethic of investing. Robin John has. In his engaging and compelling book, Robin would convince us of the moral obligations of partial ownership through our investments and of the significant impact we can have by joining together around five basic standards for ethical investing. You'll not only want to read this book but also distribute it to your friends." —Sandy Willson, pastor emeritus of the Second Presbyterian Church in Memphis, Tennessee and former interim president of The Gospel Coalition

"Robin John has written a book that will both delight and challenge faith-driven investors. John engages his readers with brisk prose, telling anecdotes, and probing questions. The book especially challenges the careless investor who dumps money into an index fund to let their assets go to firms that harm civil life. Robin John argues that since investors actually own parts of companies, they should act accordingly. He urges us to ask, 'Do my investments serve and promote the public good? Do the companies I own (however partially) treat their workers well? Relieve deep pain? Love their neighbors or exploit them? Do they create long-term and sustainable profits?' In brief, do they embrace values believers affirm? Are they the kinds of companies we hope to see succeed? If this kind of question matters to you, let this book answer those questions and help you invest according to your convictions." —Dan Doriani, PhD, professor of Biblical Theology at the Covenant Seminary and founder of the Center for Faith and Work in St. Louis

The
GOOD
INVESTOR

HOW YOUR WORK CAN
CONFRONT INJUSTICE, LOVE YOUR NEIGHBOR,
AND BRING HEALING TO THE WORLD

ROBIN JOHN

Forefront
BOOKS

Published by Forefront Books, Nashville, Tennessee.
Distributed by Simon & Schuster.

Library of Congress Control Number: 2025907139

Print ISBN: 978-1-63763-452-3
E-book ISBN: 978-1-63763-453-0

Cover Design by Bruce Gore, Gore Studio, Inc.
Interior Design by PerfecType, Nashville, TN
Printed in the United States of America

25 26 27 28 29 30 LAK 10 9 8 7 6 5 4 3 2 1

God's abundance is revealed in the imagination
and courage to see the world,
not as it is—full of injustice—
but as it could be, transformed.

JÜRGEN MOLTMANN[1]

CONTENTS

FOREWORD

I've been in the financial services industry since graduating from Indiana University with my MBA in 1967. I've worked with large firms, started my own small firm (Blue Trust), and eventually felt a strong calling to use my education and experience to assist Christians in planning and managing their finances in a manner that aligns with their spiritual aspirations and maximizes their generosity. Along with many others who worked in the company I founded, we developed a comprehensive process in Christian financial planning that integrates professional advice with biblical principles, enabling decision-making to become a way that God works in our lives and benefits the Kingdom. As I and others who share this mission began integrating biblical wisdom into professional financial advice, we quickly realized how God's Word applies universally to every financial situation, regardless of time, place, or circumstance.

Over the decades, my life's work has centered on two fundamental truths. First: God owns everything. Second:

God has invited us to be the stewards of what He owns, entrusting us with resources to use in ways that reflect His beauty or glory. These convictions have guided me as I've attempted to encourage all of us to examine our beliefs about our relationship with God. Do we really believe God owns it all—and are we willing to genuinely trust God and live as if this is true? If the answer is *yes*, we will become radically generous with all that we have, including our money.

Our generosity (or lack thereof) reveals what we really believe, and generosity is foundational to being good stewards. These principles explain why I've spent so much energy helping clients integrate biblical values into their financial planning and grow in their generosity. It's why I founded Kingdom Advisors, a network of over 3,500 financial advisors helping clients be generous stewards of God's resources. And it's why I co-founded National Christian Foundation which has mobilized more than $18 billion for 90,000 churches, ministries, and charities.

Along the way, however, we have faced a significant challenge in determining how to help people with their actual investing, helping clients invest in a way that honors our Lord and His Kingdom. The investment industry is primarily focused on maximizing returns and minimizing risk, but it fails to address crucial aspects of maximizing Kingdom impact and bringing glory to our Lord and Savior. While we've been able to help thousands of people have Kingdom impact through practicing generosity, it's been harder to help people have Kingdom impact with their investments themselves (how they earn the wealth they give away). Stewardship is about every aspect of life (God owns it all), which absolutely includes generosity but also includes the *way* we invest. There's been a gap in the connection between these two aspects of stewardship, and *The Good Investor* bridges that gap. This book provides the capstone of everything I always believed but didn't think was possible.

I firmly believe that if you don't ask the right question, you can't receive the right answer. Robin's book poses and answers the pivotal question: Can I make a values-based investment that maximizes the values I uphold? Specifically, can we make investments that glorify God and yield results that reflect sound thinking and wise decision-making? To my knowledge, this may be the first book providing a workable framework for thinking biblically about our investments and then helping us practice wisdom as we make specific investment choices. *The Good Investor* offers a scaffold for asking the right questions, and in doing so, helps us assess whether we can incorporate our values into our investments. All investors should be thinking this way.

The most effective self-help books simplify intricate challenges and questions. This book simplifies and presents a thought process and decision-making approach that will transform your perspective and how you manage your investments. Robin is a passionate executive in the investment industry with strong character and a commitment to honoring God. *The Good Investor* is thoughtful, credible, compelling, highly professional, relevant, and humble— and I recommend it for anyone who wants to honor God and have a Kingdom impact with how they steward the financial resources entrusted to them by a gracious God.

God has raised individuals like Robin in the investment industry who are passionate about their faith. Robin and his team intentionally integrate faith and purpose into their processes and decision-making, and you'll discover this in these pages. This book is not prescriptive, but more importantly, transformational. Everyone should read this book.

Ron Blue
Founder of Kingdom Advisors, Co-Founder of National Christian Foundation, and author of God Owns It All, Mastering Your Money, *and numerous other books*

FIRST WORD

This is a book about joy, specifically the joy that comes from making the world good. This is also a book about investing. Maybe it seems odd to see *joy* and *investing* next to one another. Investing easily evokes images of greedy tycoons pillaging resources and communities for their own selfish interests. Hollywood (consider *Wall Street, Boiler Room, The Wolf of Wall Street,* just for starters) regularly portrays investors choosing to hurt others as they advance themselves, and Hollywood certainly has lots of material to work with. Even at its best, we often imagine investing as only concerned with a narrow sphere: our individual need to manage security for our family and our future.

But what if investing holds a far more potent capacity: the potential for creative, generative good? What if investing can help us address our own genuine financial needs while at the same time confronting injustice, loving our neighbors, and healing some of the world's crushing pain? What if investing has a higher calling: to serve the common good and to be an engine of blessing? To be a path to joy?

I hope that in the pages to follow, you'll discover more about how your faith, values, and passions can be expressed through your investments and make significant impact. I know I've found new energy and inspiration as I've discovered how these pieces of our everyday life (whether we recognize it or not) carry the potential to do immense good. I hope you will find your own thread of joy in all this like I have. As Alfred, Lord Tennyson wrote, "Come, my friends, 'tis not too late to seek a newer world."[2]

Your life and your financial decisions *can* make a significant impact. We are not talking about abstract ethical ideas but realities grounded in the concrete experiences I have had in my life on two sides of the world: from a childhood in a small village in India to leading a US investment firm that manages billions of dollars in assets.

I have seen beauty and sorrow in my life, and I have been offered overwhelming grace and mercy, which has stirred the ache in my heart for a better world. I hope that as you hear how this longing grew in me that you'll find it growing in you, too, and that it will shape the way you approach your work and your money as it did for me.

How Beautiful the World Could Be

1

A Vision of Hope

> *One evening, when we were already resting on the floor of our hut, dead tired, soup bowls in hand, a fellow prisoner rushed in and asked us to run out to the assembly grounds and see the wonderful sunset. Standing outside we saw sinister clouds glowing in the west and the whole sky alive with clouds of ever-changing shapes and colors, from steel blue to blood red. The desolate grey mud huts provided a sharp contrast, while the puddles on the muddy ground reflected the glowing sky. Then, after minutes of moving silence, one prisoner said to another, "How beautiful the world could be."*
>
> Viktor E. Frankl[3]

Growing up in the tiny village of Kangazha—tucked into the south Indian state of Kerala—my younger brother Sony and I had seen a plane only once. I had stared into the sky, mouth agape as the jet shrank smaller and smaller, an ant swallowed by clouds of white. I couldn't imagine what kind of people would be riding in such a thing or where these people could possibly be going.

Now, twenty years later, I boarded one of those flying ants to return to India courtesy of my employer Mellon Bank.[4] I had landed a back-office temp job with Mellon when I was in college at Tufts, working with income collections. The temp position turned permanent, and eventually the bank asked me to move back to India to help set up their operations in Pune. So, twenty-four years old and very green, I was en route to Mumbai to do important work. Exhilarating.

I stepped onto the KLM 747 from the jetway at Logan Airport, and the stewardess in cerulean blue glanced at my boarding pass, smiled, and gestured for me to turn left. The few times I'd flown, I'd always followed the long queue right. Wide-eyed, I rolled my carry-on through the veil into first class. Each seat held small gifts tucked into a stylish bag, and Dutch chefs prepared gourmet food (apple tartelettes, asparagus, salmon with couscous, and tiny chocolates) served on delft blue plates. The big shocker was how every seat laid out into a bed with a cozy blanket and fluffy pillow. I had no idea people stretched out and slept like babies while hurtling across the globe at 35,000 feet.

When I stepped out of the Mumbai International Airport, I was hit by a wave of scorching heat—thick and humid—and the sound of roaring engines and honking cars that resonated with complete madness. A crowd of people moved and pressed together, chaotic, like the swirling movement of thousands of birds in the sky.

A putrid wave, like sweat and decay accented by jasmine, assaulted me. Reflexively, I covered my nose with my hand. Alongside the runways, a slum of makeshift dwellings of thousands of workers and families overran the vacant acres—castoff bricks, scraps of aluminum and blue tarp all stitched together with rope, discarded lumber, and duct tape. There was no plumbing and no disposal system for trash. The residents *depended* on the rancid refuse.

Nobel Prize winner Katherine Boo described the harsh reality:

> Every morning, thousands of waste-pickers fanned out across the airport area in search of vendible excess—a few pounds of the eight thousand tons of garbage that Mumbai was extruding daily. These scavengers darted after crumpled cigarette packs tossed from cars with tinted windows. They dredged sewers and raided dumpsters for empty bottles of water and beer. Each evening, they returned down the slum road with gunny sacks of garbage on their backs, like a procession of broken-toothed, profit-minded Santas.[5]

So, yes, imagine the smell. I was sobered by the sight as I stepped into the chauffeured black SUV, driving right past them. Though my family had left when I was eight, India remained my motherland. But Kerala—verdant and green, spacious with blue skies, a place where you could breathe deep—was nothing like this. Kerala is so beautiful that many Indians refer to it as "God's own country." People didn't have much, but you didn't need much there either.

I spent my first night at the Grand Hyatt, a five-star hotel with marble floors, water fountains, and tall, lighted pillars. My palatial room had a king size bed with 400-thread-count Egyptian cotton sheets and windows overlooking the clear aqua pool in the courtyard encircled by palm trees. Paradise.

And my goodness, the food. As a kid, after we moved from India to Boston, our family rarely ate out, visiting the Indian buffet only on special occasions and getting Whoppers at Burger King only when we had buy-one-get-one-free coupons. After college, I'd gather with a few friends, purchase a loaf of bread and rotisserie chicken from the grocery store, and share dinner in the parking lot. But here I was at a table with candles and white linens and servers wearing black-tie attire eagerly attending to my every whim. I stared at the menu. *How in the world does anyone afford to eat here?* But I had the company credit card, so I ordered a plate overflowing with jumbo prawns and green mint biryani. I'd eaten biryani my whole life, but *mint* biryani—a revelation.

Inside the hotel, everything was pristine, bliss. Most everyone looked like models for commercials or magazine covers, enjoying dazzling food and ordering drinks poolside.

Outside the hotel, most of the people looked disheveled and worn, worked over, as though they were carrying a century's sorrows. I saw blind children begging (many of them purposefully blinded by their keepers so they'd be more profitable) and a man with bloody knees, dragging himself across gravel and concrete.

Inside was heaven; outside was hell.

I had no idea how to process this reality—those slums we'd driven past as I rode in plush comfort protected from the stench and heat to the wonders I'd experienced aboard that flying resort on the way to the chilled high-rise of ease and joy. In one hour, I encountered two poles: the astounding beauty humans create *and* the squalor humans often suffer.

It wasn't the disparity that was most perplexing but the fact that no one on the inside seemed to even pause to consider the outside. There was one universe this side of the glass doors and an entirely separate universe on the other.

AMAL AND KAMAL

The next morning, my driver drove me three hours to Pune, a city of nearly four million. Security waved us into a gated community where a brick driveway led to a gorgeous crisp white two-story home with a covered porch and a clay-red tiled roof. Amal, the housekeeper, and Kamal, the cook, greeted me at the door with toothy grins and grabbed my bags.

"Welcome, sir, welcome." They flashed big smiles, bowed, and ushered me inside with a barrage of politeness. "Sir, welcome, sir. Sir, would you like a drink? Sir, what can we get you?" I asked them to please call me Robin, but they just smiled and kept piling on the sirs.

Amal and Kamal were from a village forty-five minutes away, working in Pune so they could send money home. Though they were only in their twenties (like me), they ran the house like seasoned butlers. Amal made my bed and ironed my clothes. Every morning, Kamal would ask, "Sir, what would you like for breakfast?" Again, at dinner: "Sir, what would you like to eat?" Always followed by, "What can I get you, sir?" And "Sir, eat more, sir." I tried to keep it simple and healthy: roti, chicken tandoori, dahl, and any vegetable they wanted to make. But I couldn't resist Kamal's gulab jamun, a confectionary of soft dough soaked in sweet syrup.

The house had five bedrooms, each with a king bed, lush sheets, a private bathroom with a tub and tiled shower, and individual Hitachi air-conditioners dialed into each guest's preferred temperature. Usually though, most of those rooms were empty. Another Mellon employee, Justin, came for short periods, but most weeks it was just me, Amal, and Kamal. The guest areas and the communal living room all enjoyed cool air—but not the spaces intended only for house staff. My refrigerated bedroom always beckoned, but I enjoyed my housemates and often joined them in the steaming kitchen to talk. When Kamal cooked, the oven glowed and radiated like a small sun. I offered to chop vegetables or set the table, but they always met my offers with waves of the hand and protest.

"Sir, no, sir."

One evening, as we chatted in our sauna doubling as a kitchen, I glanced into the adjacent pantry and for the first time noticed a small mat made of Korai grass.

"Is this where you sleep?"

"Yes," they answered.

I opened the door wider and peered inside. Shelves of canned food and stacks of white dishes and bags of rice. And two thin grass mats—no pillow, no blanket, no airflow. Just cramped quarters and heat.

"This is terrible," I exclaimed, my intensity jolting them. "You can't live like this. You need to stay in one of the bedrooms."

"No, sir," they answered. "No, sir." Their bodies tensed; panic flooded their eyes.

This was ludicrous. We had a house full of vacant rooms—and two men crammed into a furnace of a pantry without even rudimentary bedding.

Disturbed, I would have asked Justin what to do, as he had been with the company much longer than me. However, Justin had already made it clear that Amal and Kamal were nuisances. One evening, Justin and I were in the living room when the front door opened, and Kamal walked in. Justin watched Kamal with narrowed eyes and clenched jaw, like a teacher annoyed at having to tell his pupil yet *again* that 2+2=4.

"Servants," Justin said, "should not use the front door." Then he walked out.

Kamal's shoulders slumped. He stood staring a hole into the floor.

My brain went foggy. I couldn't pull out any words. *What just happened?*

After a few agonizing moments, Kamal looked up, his eyes moist and heavy. He seemed smaller, as if his soul had drained of air and light.

"Sir," he said quietly, "I am a human being too."

Justin's words pierced me. I didn't feel different from Kamal or Amal. I looked like them and had an accent like them. If only a few things had gone differently for me, I, too, could have been sleeping on a mat in the pantry and being told to enter through the back.

When I saw the conditions Kamal and Amal lived in, I knew I'd get no help from Justin. Instead, angry and reeling, I emailed HR back in Boston. "This is inhumane," I wrote.

"This is wrong and has to change." A flurry of communication led nowhere. They said the guesthouse was outsourced, and the staff were not their employees, which was true. They said they had no control over the situation, which wasn't exactly true. A heavyweight operation, my company wielded serious clout. If they decided to raise the issue with their vendor and insisted on better conditions, things would have changed. Fast. But my company didn't see intervention as an option. They weren't malicious or evil. They simply operated on one side of those glass doors. And unfortunately, Amal and Kamal happened to exist on the other side. Different universes. Nothing could be done. That's just the way business works, just the way the world works.

But does it have to? That year in India, and especially my months living with Amal and Kamal, raised unexpected questions that needled me, pushing and prodding. What is the purpose of work and business? And do my faith and values have anything to say to that purpose? Is it simply to maximize profits even at the expense of people like Amal and Kamal?

On one hand, I saw how business could harness society's massive ingenuity to lift people out of poverty. I had young college graduates on my team still living in the slums who were feeling immense hope for their family's future because of their new career at Mellon. On the other hand, I saw how businesses were mistreating the poor all around me from children to the very elderly. I wondered how we could use business as a more powerful engine of blessing to make our world more just and whole.

Is it possible for a company and its investors to make a good profit *and* make a good world?

For me as a Christian, an immensely important query emerged over the next few years as I continued to work out the implications of these experiences: How can my life embrace what Mary Clark Moschella describes as "the imagination and courage to see the world, not as it is—full of injustice—but as it could be, transformed"?[6]

These are the questions I want to ponder with you, questions that emerge from my own story. What I'm really hoping for, though, is that as you hear a little bit about how I came to see the possibilities of using investments to make the world better that it will spark new energy and imagination in your own story, work, and places of influence.

I have regrets about my experience in Pune. Though internally I identified with Kamal and Amal, I did have power there, only I didn't use my power well. I wish I'd done more.

I write as a Christian, but my hope is that most of us, regardless of worldview, would agree that a just world, overflowing with mercy and humility, would be a very, very good world.

THE IMPACT OF OUR LIFE AND WORK

My engine runs on hope—a realistic hope, but full-brimmed nonetheless. In my work as the cofounder of an investment firm, I've seen immense creativity, innovation, sacrifice, and resourcefulness. I've experienced how businesses—and the leaders who with sweat, grit, and savvy build those businesses—ignite extraordinary momentum that has the power to lift people out of poverty, cure diseases, and confront alarming crises such as famine, drought, and ecological disaster. I have friends who, only a decade ago, would have buried their child if it hadn't been for a biotechnology company's astounding tenacity.

However, uncoupled from a vision for the common good and a profound love of neighbor, powers intended to heal and renew can instead pillage and destroy. My experience in Pune offers merely one personal anecdote, hinting at systemic ills. How many drug companies have gouged prices or juiced their research or profited from customers getting hooked on their "medicine"? How many financial institutions have pushed mortgages and pumped speculative schemes that lined their pockets while leaving retirees and young families in the lurch? How many corporations have touted their commitment to integrity only to be caught cooking the figures and covering up transgressions?

Villains like Enron, Theranos, or Bernie Madoff are easily burned in effigy. We all know the harm they've done, and none of them get invited to the neighborhood BBQ. What's far more complicated is how often noble potential lies fallow not because of malevolent intent but simply because we're unaware.

Many of us assume we're too insignificant or have too few resources or possess too little knowledge to have any impact on these global forces. We hear the news of corporate malfeasance or international sex trafficking or an industry's racial bias, and we believe we are irrelevant, helpless. We're trapped on one side of the door with no recourse, no way to help.

Yet none of us are helpless. I believe that small, seemingly insignificant people making small, everyday decisions have massive ripple effects far beyond anything we see.

Ammachi, my grandmother (*Ammachi* is the word for *grandmother* in Malayalam, my family's native language.), was tiny, only 4' 6" tall. She married my grandfather (Appacha) when she was young, and they had eight children. She spoke few words, but I still hear the echoes of her life and her love. Her early years were grit-and-bone survival. Often, Ammachi would brush away food, insisting she wasn't hungry and making sure everyone else's plate had a spoonful of rice or beans. Due to malnutrition, her legs shriveled and bowed, squeezing another inch or two from her frail frame.

But her love—what rich and strong love. Even now, when I return to the village, neighbors talk about my Ammachi. They stop to tell me how she always took care of others, always checked on those who were struggling, and always made sure everyone had the essentials. On a recent visit, neighbors insisted I come and sit on their porch. They were ailing and bent over, but they smiled wide and told me old tales about my family and especially my grandmother, stories like the ones I've heard many times. How she somehow scraped together a few rupees for a neighbor when they had no way to pay a bill. How she dropped off vegetables when a family's cupboard was bare. How she would appear on the doorstep when there was grief or sorrow and just sit in silence. Ammachi was a cord, holding the community together.

My grandmother would never have imagined her life as having any great impact, but the stories tell a different truth. Ammachi had so little, but somehow her little multiplied like loaves and fishes. Grace emanated from her. When you were with Ammachi, you felt less alone, less afraid.

Ammachi taught me, with her steadiness and her sacrificial love, that caring for others is our responsibility. This is true even when our resources are meager and even though the need is mammoth. Our job, Ammachi taught me, is to be faithful to do our part; the results are out of our hands. If we're thrust upon a vast desert with only a thimble of water, then that one thimble will have to do. Ammachi, with her little thimble of life, taught me this.

In my parents' dining room in Boston, a family portrait hangs on the wall. All of us are there dressed up and trying to hold natural smiles as the photographer cajoles us to say "cheese." I'm always drawn to Ammachi's face. I see her watching over me. I see in her wrinkled face and slouched body a lifetime of giving and generosity. I see in that one kind gaze a long, faithful story of profound love and selfless concern for others.

Recently, a cousin gave me my grandfather's Bible. Appacha was a pastor with far-reaching influence. He was responsible for helping trailblaze a wing of the Pentecostal church within a region of Kerala and mobilizing ministries to serve the poor. Appacha's Bible has scribbles throughout the margins, verses underlined, and numerous cross-references. I'm immensely grateful to have it. However, my mom once said, "You should have asked for your grandmother's Bible instead of your grandfather's."

"Why?" I asked.

"Appacha's Bible is filled with notes," Mom answered. "Ammachi's is filled with tears."

From those tears grew a powerful legacy. Ammachi gave what she had. And both her love and her actions changed her little portion of the world.

Often, changing the big world starts with small and ordinary steps toward change. Whenever I see her warm face in that picture, whenever I see and hear Ammachi in my mind and heart, I know I'm now responsible to follow her example.

So, what if it isn't true that we're powerless? What if it isn't true that our little choices have no impact on the world around us? Our everyday decisions can make the world more what we long for it to be, more what *God* longs for it to be. And something most of us do already (investing) can participate in the world's healing. The allocation of capital is a powerful tool; when used thoughtfully, and in connection with its true purpose, investing can create immense value and solve some of the world's deepest needs. Or, when disconnected from its true purpose, it can extract value and cause extensive damage.

One unique reality about my form of work is that most of us, at some level, engage in it. *The Washington Post* reports that 61 percent of Americans participate in the stock market in some way.[7] Only a handful of us might be a carpenter or teacher or attorney or a stay-at-home parent, but most of us are in one way or another investors. We might have a retirement account we rarely remember or an inheritance to figure out or a large, sophisticated portfolio, but whichever, we are investors. Our money is doing work in the world. The question is whether our money is doing work that harms or work that helps. My hope as you read my story is that you will find inspiration to imagine how your investments can do good, how your investments can help and heal.

The possibilities for doing good, bringing power to bear on behalf of those most in need of relief, gives me hope. We're *not* helpless. Our investments, our lives and work, our resolve to challenge the status quo—these are seeds of beauty.

Imagine how beautiful the world could be.

Investing Our Lives for the World's Joy

Ponder your work, your investing, and your daily lifestyle choices. Are there any small (or large) ways you may be passively allowing exploitation? Are there any ways you are ignoring harm done to others or any places where you've been discouraged to act because you assumed you couldn't make a difference?

Out From Eden

2

Investing that Works

> *May the virtue of our daily work*
> *Hallow our nightly prayers.*
>
> Celtic Daily Prayers[8]

On my eighth birthday, my family packed up everything we could cram into our suitcases and flew out of the Cochin International Airport for what seemed like a million miles to New York. My uncle C. M. Titus, one of the pastors at Boston's Tremont Baptist Temple (a church with a history tied to the Underground Railroad and the abolitionists), picked us up at JFK Airport in the church van. Those first hours on the drive to Boston are a blur, but I remember sitting in the van's back row, staring wide-eyed at the sky-scrapers and the infinite paved roads and noticing how everything, even the rushing traffic, seemed orderly. What strange, remarkable planet was this?

My uncle pulled into a Roy Rogers, eager to introduce us to the wonders of the American cheeseburger. I unwrapped the greasy paper and bit into odd meat and gummy bread, oozing with some unidentifiable sauce. I choked and swallowed, re-wrapped the burger, and stuffed it underneath my seat.

Over the decade that followed, I worked hard to assimilate into my new country and culture. The early years were difficult because I was still learning English, but I loved school and thrived in high school. I attended Tufts University, and after graduating, found my first big corporate job at Mellon, as I mentioned in the last chapter. I was so unnerved by how the business world worked that I resigned. I landed another finance job, but a perplexing round of office politics led to my manager firing me within just a few months. At twenty-six years old, I was unemployed, living in my parents' basement.

Humiliated, I maintained my familiar routine so that my parents wouldn't suspect anything was wrong. I left the house in slacks and a dress shirt at 8:00 sharp each morning. I drove less than a mile to Tufts Library where I sat among the stacks, using the public computers and *The Boston Globe* to search for jobs. At 6:00, I drove home.

During these months playing work, I faced an existential crisis. What was I doing with my life? I yearned to participate in something meaningful, for my life to be caught up in the big story of God's love for the world. Instead, I was spinning my wheels, overdressed in the public library forty hours a week. I wanted my whole life to have meaning. I wanted my work itself to have purpose. Late every night, I sat in prayer on the concrete basement floor by the washer and dryer and found encouragement from the words of Psalm 1:

> Blessed is the one who does not walk in step with the wicked or stand in the way that sinners take or sit in the company of mockers, but whose delight is in the law of the LORD, and who meditates on his law day and night. That person is like a tree planted by streams of water, which yields its fruit in season and whose leaf does not wither—whatever they do prospers. (NIV)

The words of this psalm gave me comfort that by delighting in the Lord and meditating on His Word, He would direct and sustain me. I can be blessed and prosperous even without walking in step with the wicked, and even by pursuing a life that fully delights in the law of God. I wasn't necessarily expecting some sort of financial prosperity, but I believed and trusted that whatever prosperity God promises in His Word is good for me.

Early on, I was misguided in how to pursue this vision. For years—before I graduated from Tufts and then again before I took the bank job—I would pray for a call from God to go into the ministry. I was entrenched in a false idea, rampant in some areas of Christian culture (especially at that time), that overt Christian activities such as being a pastor or missionary provided the only real opportunities for truly meaningful spiritual work. So, I prayed and pleaded for that mystical call. Now as I found myself without a job and again wondering if I should have gone into ministry, I cried out to God. Sitting alone in my parents' basement beside those rusty appliances, my grasping prayer for a purpose fed off the presumption that to participate in God's work in the world, I needed to receive "the call" to "genuine ministry." Other vocations were fine, even respectable (especially as they provided the means to give money away to those doing the truly valuable work), but undeniably second tier. In my church setting, even the phrase "the man of God" was reserved for those in pastoral vocation.

Most Christians are not in formal Christian ministry, but like many, I had the distorted idea that anything else would not be in direct connection with service to God. I longed to be first tier in serving God's purposes. So, I started part-time seminary classes, hoping that somehow that environment would trigger the divine hand. I kept pleading. But all I heard was silence. *Well,* I thought, dejected and confused, *I don't have a calling, so I guess I'll just make money and support those who do.*

A WORKING GOD

As I meditated on the Bible's creation story, my own understanding of the word *work* was transformed. I began to see that all work is intended to reflect God.

Genesis opens the story of the world by showing us God at work. Like a potter at the wheel or a carpenter laying frame, God is engrossed in His labor. He is engaged in every imaginable kind of work. The Original Architect unveils the first flashes of His design, pulling back creation's dark curtain to reveal the flickering marvel: light. And then with a sigh of contentment, God offers one word: "Good."

The Cosmic Engineer gathers molecules and particles from the vast reaches, creating huge mountains of earth and filling deep valleys with flowing, life-giving water. Again, with great delight, God says, "Good."

The Great Farmer turns the rich, black soil into a bounty of goodness: ruby red raspberries, plump pears, sweet corn, and butternut squash.

"Good," God says.

Then, in a burst of creativity, God rolls up His sleeves and fashions wonders. Sun, moon, and stars shimmer and burn. Billions of creatures, giant blue whales and tiny hummingbirds, spill into the seas and over the land. We stand in awe now at the diverse spectacle traced back to those original creative acts: water buffaloes and Arabian leopards, scarlet kingsnakes and glass frogs, macaroni penguins and flying squirrels. My son Christian and I enjoy looking at pictures of funny-looking creatures like the naked mole rat and the blobfish. We don't understand why God created some of these creatures, but after making each one, with pure delight, He gives that same refrain: "Good. Good. Good."

Finally, as if summoning the deepest resources of energy and imagination, the true Worker-Artist created other worker-artists who would be like Him and who would carry His very life and image in their own bodies. God's voice spoke words that still resound with force and wonder:

> Then God said, "Let us make mankind in our image, in our likeness, so that they may rule over the fish in the sea and the birds in the sky, over the livestock and all the wild animals, and over all the creatures that move along the ground." So God created mankind in his own image, in the image of God he created them; male and female he created them. (Genesis 1:26–27 NIV)

In this climactic creative act, God breathed life into humans, humans who would carry on God's *work*. This is essential: Woman and man were from the beginning created to work alongside God. Co-creators. This time, with unbridled joy and satisfaction, God adds a word: "Very good."

But there's an even more stunning wrinkle in the Genesis story: God got His work started—but then God handed the work off to us. God made *His* work *our* work. In fact, God created us in His image and in His nature *so that* He can trust us with His work and so that we can reflect God in our work. God was the first Gardener, but then God made *all* of us gardeners. Immediately after His pinnacle act of bringing humans into the world, God passed Adam and Eve a job description: "Prosper! Reproduce! Fill Earth! Take charge! Be responsible for fish in the sea and birds in the air, for every living thing that moves on the face of Earth" (Genesis 1:28 MSG).

Nurturing and tending creation—what had until then been uniquely God's domain—would now be Adam and Eve's undertaking. God did not place Adam and Eve in the Garden of Eden merely to roam carefree, playing croquet and stuffing themselves with figs and pomegranates. They had work to do. And this work was inherently *good*.

Even more fascinating is how God intentionally left the creative work unfinished. The whole earth was not yet filled with flourishing goodness. The Garden of Eden was only a small portion of God's original creation, with everything outside its boundary (the rest of the wild planet) still uninhabited and unruly.[9] Eden was only the starting point, the prototype, revealing the lush bounty God desired to eventually extend everywhere.[10] Remember, Adam and Eve were to be fruitful and nurture the world toward abundance because the world was not yet fruitful, not yet abundant.

In fact, the land was wondrous but still a little—can we say it?—*bare*. Genesis provides two reasons the Garden was not yet enjoying its full potential: God hadn't sent rain to nourish the soil, but also "there was no one to work the ground" (Genesis 2:5 NIV). In a generous move that might even seem to us a bit reckless, God had designed the world to need humans. God made us all gardeners, all of us responsible to tend, nurture, and extend God's beautiful Eden everywhere. We have essential work to do. And this work is immensely *good*.

The world is good. Creation is good. Humans are good. And—we must not miss this—work itself (including the work of investments required to fuel every kind of business) is *good*. Of course, the story turns dark from here. Still, this is where the story begins: in unqualified, lavish goodness. And this goodness—though we'll mar the beauty and though God will have to rescue us from our calamity—is never obliterated. And God, echoing this story, still asks humans to do these good, necessary tasks. There's so much work to do.

THE SEARCH

Those nights beside the clanking appliances in my parents' basement transitioned to weekly meetings with my brother

Sony and our friend Finny Kuruvilla. The three of us began meeting on Wednesday nights at Finny's Cambridge apartment. We all had something in common: We were all at a crossroads in our careers, seeking God's leading for how to align our faith with our daily work.

At first, we kept focusing narrowly on "Christian ministry," either starting a retreat center or a religious nonprofit. But over time, as we met and prayed, our ideas and vision expanded. Finny especially had the wildest ideas. He came in excited one night: We'd create a company that made milk from *oats*! Finny might as well have suggested we figure out how to levitate. Another night, in early 2008, his revolutionary idea was that we would create hamburgers *without using meat*!

Conditioned to his vegan evangelism, I rolled my eyes. Finny floated these ideas in January 2008, and he enjoys reminding me how in the decade that followed, both Impossible Foods and Beyond Meat (meatless burgers) launched, valued in the billions. And in 2021, Oatly (milk from oats) went public, valued at more than $10 billion.

We considered starting a consulting firm to develop bioinformatic algorithms. We briefly researched starting a vegan fast-food franchise, even going as far as testing recipes in our own kitchens to share and rate. We pondered launching our own pharmaceutical company. With all of this, we were searching for ideas that could do real social good while also making us a good living.

For a while, Finny had been seriously investigating investing in the stock market, but the process was difficult because whenever he looked at mutual funds and scanned the companies those funds were purchasing, he always felt uneasy. Many of the companies were not businesses he'd ever want to own or be involved with (corporations that he considered predatory or bad for society or the environment). Profiting from these companies would contradict so many of his principles and so many of his commitments to justice and basic morality. Finny explained how, because of these concerns, he'd started choosing individual companies to invest in on his own. "How could I make money from something I believe is bad?" he said.

Although I had never invested until this point in my life, I was intrigued, and we started a little investment club to occupy our untapped energy while we continued to labor over our big question about our future. Finny, Sony, and I pooled together a few thousand dollars, pored over corporate documents, and bought a handful of shares.

One afternoon, I asked Finny, "Do you think there are a lot of people who want to align their values and their investments?" That question lit a beacon. Surely there were everyday folks like us trying to live by ethical principles who had no idea that they were in fact supporting and profiting from the very things they opposed through their 401(k)s or IRAs. And most people didn't have the time to research individual companies. We began to dream about the massive transformation that could happen if just a small percentage of us collectively directed our investments to companies who were doing good in the world.

I still shake my head at the whirlwind that unleashed. All our other business ideas quickly faded. I spent two weeks around Christmas with a pile of books from the library, studying stocks, the brokerage business, banking, and portfolio management. By May, we started our own investment company, Eventide Asset Management. Finny's wife, Laura, suggested the name *Eventide*, which means "evening" in old English. The name seemed perfect, especially as I read John 9:4, which calls on God's people to be diligent to work while the daylight ebbs before the night descends. In these ancient words, we heard the call to put our hands to what needs to be done while there is still daylight to do it, to join God's healing work in the world even if at times the light seems to be fading. Interestingly, Mother Teresa and Mahatma Gandhi's favorite old English hymn was "Abide with Me, Fast Falls the Eventide," and the Indian army would march to the hymn annually during the Indian Republic Day.

But we weren't fading. We were at warp speed. It was May, and we had plans to open a public mutual fund in July. And we were so green. In March 2008, Finny wrote me an email, explaining how he'd just ordered two books from Amazon:

> One is on how to create and run a mutual fund. We're going to have to scour that book very carefully. My estimation is that we're going to have to do a lot of reading in the next four months. I should be able to read for at least 1 hour / day. Robin, if you could plan to read 3 hours / day, then between both of us we can know all that we'll need to pull this off.

We had a range of industry knowledge and the technical skills needed to identify and evaluate companies. But creating and managing a mutual fund, with all the bureaucratic red tape, was a whole other beast. We had to create an Everest-sized pile of documents—LLC operating agreement, compliance documents, an extensive business plan, a bulky mutual fund prospectus, and a Statement of Additional Information—all just to get the ball rolling.

We decided Finny would oversee the investments, and I would oversee sales, marketing, compliance, and operations. However, certain sections required legal expertise, and neither of us had that. When I received our first bill from the attorneys, the amount was staggering. I went into the law firm's office, hat in hand, and negotiated an 80 percent reduction on the outstanding bill we owed. I don't know if they agreed because they had mercy on us or because they just assumed we'd never make it and wanted to at least get something before the whole thing went bust.

I drained my life savings ($70,000) and pooled it with what Finny and I and a few other friends and family members scraped together. I was risking everything, dumping my last dollar into Eventide, a job that we hoped would be able to pay me $10,000 that first year. The move wouldn't have worried me much except for the fact that my fiancé Jaunita was finishing nursing school, and we were getting married in November. We couldn't fail.

I hit the road, hustling to find investors, and after we were married, Jaunita faithfully spent hours on the road with me. To save money, we ate at Mexican restaurants with free chips and salsa, and we ordered one meal to share, always asking for extra tortillas. My rule was as long as the motel had a door facing inside and cost less than $50, it was fine. Generally, this rule worked for us. But once in 2009, we walked into a dingy, smoke-infested room, and I didn't think we'd last. I wrapped t-shirts around the grimy pillows and somehow, we made it through the night. The next morning, Jaunita joined me for a meeting with a group of financial advisors in Johnson City, Tennessee. We'd only planned for a one-hour meeting, but we spent a chunk of the day with them, and they even took Jaunita and me out to lunch. That visit was monumental, as they became some of our earliest clients.

That first year, we racked up debt on our credit card (including most of our wedding expenses). I scoured Craigslist for part-time jobs. I explored working with an airline, mainly for the free travel that I could then use to visit potential investors. Finny emailed me information on a research group paying $1,000 to participants in a sleep study. "Seems like a good deal," Finny said. Unfortunately, I didn't qualify for the sleep study because they found that I was not a healthy sleeper.

All these concerted efforts seemed absolutely worth the risk because Eventide was something I believed in. This work mattered. I had a purpose. I could envision how we could be part of an important movement, helping people do good work with their money.

Still, though, I continued to meet stiff resistance to the conviction that everyday work (not to mention the work of investing) carried inherent, noble value. During our second year of starting Eventide, an Indian pastor who was a friend of our family visited to preach at our church. After the service, he asked me, "Moné, moné (*son, son*), what are you doing for God?" Eagerly, I began to unfold the story of our company and how we were helping people use their money to do good—but I only got out the first sentence or two. "No, no," he said, interrupting. "I want to know what you're doing for *God*."

There were lots of ways I could have answered that would have made him smile and pat my shoulder with fatherly affection. I could have regaled him with my stories of going on a foreign mission trip to Tanzania (I mean, *two* whole weeks). I could have explained how I taught in the church's Sunday School or served as the youth leader. But I chose to talk to him about what I did Monday to Friday, serving God with investing. And he brushed it away. It was irrelevant to him.

And even as I attempted to explain our investing enterprise, I could have led with how our company business plan included donating the majority of profits to serve the poor, or with the fact that many of our investors would give away much of their profits to Christian causes and to the poor. Then he would have nodded with delight. But that wasn't the *point*. I believed that investing *itself*, marshaling resources and capital to nurture wholeness and shalom, could count as God-honoring work. The ways I spent most of the energy and hours of my life—the myriad of ways I hoped to be contributing to and loving God's world—those things were intrinsically valuable. Those things were of themselves *good*.

The earliest chapters of Genesis make it clear that our work is good all by itself, without need for any other justification. God even gives them something like a commissioning service and points out the many resources He has provided, inviting humanity to join Him in transforming the world into one that is alive, joyful, abundant, productive, nourishing, and beautiful. In fact, God's Genesis work included exactly the sorts of things we often, with a dismissive wave, label *secular.* The Bible depicts Adam and Eve doing good work without any churches to preach in, any under-resourced communities to serve, or any non-Christians to evangelize.

Like this pastor who brushed me aside, we often think our work is merely work. Our work, we believe, is just the unfortunate way we must make a living while we wait for relief or wait to do something else that matters in our fringe hours or waning years. We pray for retirement (a concept not found in the Bible) so we can stop working and then maybe we can do something to serve God. What an impoverished vision of the nobility of our work.

In her provocative collection of essays *Letters to a Diminished Church,* Dorothy Sayers (one of the vanguards of British detective fiction who also wrote religious essays) makes the point plain: "In nothing has the Church so lost her hold on reality as in her failure to understand and respect the secular vocation. She has allowed work and religion to become separate departments."[11] And in so doing, Sayers says that we fail to honor and promote the nobility (and God-given *responsibility*) in all kinds of work.

But praying night after night, in company with friends or alongside the washing machine, and reading the Scriptures I found so invigorating, I felt God peeling back the layers of misunderstanding that had prevented me from hearing His call for my life. God gently pointed out to me that if all the vast amounts of work that we humans do every single day is not an integral part of His great project for human flourishing, then what a pointless, despairing existence we all would be forced to live. And how can Jesus' audacious claim that He is Lord over every speck of our lives be reconciled with such an impoverished vision?

"How can anyone remain interested in a religion which seems to have no concern with nine-tenths of his life?" Sayers complained. "The Church's approach to an intelligent carpenter is usually confined to exhorting him not to be drunk and disorderly in his leisure hours, and to come to church on Sundays. What the Church should be telling him is this: that the very first demand that his religion makes upon him is that he should make good tables."[12]

We should make good tables. And write good books. And sell good insurance. And construct good bridges. And research good cures. And write good public policy. And create good technology. And teach our children virtue and joy. And take good photographs. And write good code. And serve good, nourishing meals. And invest in businesses that themselves do good. We should do all of it in God's name. *Good. Good. Good.*

Since God does work that He calls *good*, we learn that it's our duty as God's image-bearers to *also* do good work. In Psalm 8 (ISV), David made a bold declaration, telling us that God has given humans "dominion over the work of [God's] hands." God has taken His work and made it *our* work. Most of us don't think this way. This isn't our framework for how we think about ourselves—that God has crowned us with glory and honor and given us responsibility for continuing His work.

Recently, my family went to Italy. I stood in awe of so many astounding pieces of art. In Florence, Michelangelo's David overwhelmed me. I couldn't begin to imagine how human hands could craft from stone something with such intricacy, such detail. Can you imagine Michelangelo saying, "Hey, Robin, I'm going to put you in charge of the work of my hands"? That would be crazy. But God does exactly this. Only with a major difference: God empowers us for work.

Someone, as the story goes, once asked Reformer Martin Luther what he would do if he knew the world were ending tomorrow. Without missing a beat, he answered, "I'd plant a tree today." That's revolutionary.

God had to intervene—to *work*—for the world to come into being. And now God says we must work so that goodness continues to fill the world. In Psalm 104:14–15 (NIV), King David says that God creates "plants for people to cultivate—bringing forth food from the earth: wine that gladdens human hearts, oil to make their faces shine, and bread that sustains their hearts." Oil doesn't just drip out of a coconut or olive. Wine doesn't just drip out of a grape. Bread doesn't just sprout from grain. God uses human work, human cultivation, to bring about what the world needs from God's creation. We are partnering with God to care for the world, to provide for the world. This is our work.

Once the light flickered on, it was as if the whole world was illuminated. Work is good all on its own. As Jeff Van Duzer argues in his excellent book, *Why Business Matters to God*, work has *intrinsic* value and is not only worthwhile because of what it provides (i.e., money to live on or give away). Work itself is good, essential.

I had many jobs growing up, including when Sony and I started a paper route, tossing *The Boston Globe* and dodging the spray from an astonishing number of skunks on those early mornings. However, the intrinsic value of work was brought home to me when I was sixteen and stocking shelves at CVS.

I worked with Olga, the pharmacy's gray-haired matron, who greeted customers with her kind but no-nonsense directness. Olga was the steady voice of calm in an often-chaotic environment staffed with a revolving door of short-term employees. A couple of years ago, I visited my old store, and there was Olga behind the cash register wearing her blue and red CVS fleece. "I can't believe you're still here," I said. "Have you ever thought about retiring?"

She looked at me like I'd suggested she fly to the moon. "Why would I do that? I enjoy my work. How else would I spend my time that's any better?"

Many of us think of our jobs primarily as the means (or the barrier) to reaching that golden retirement date—and the earlier the better. Others use their jobs like a piece on a chess board, jumping from job to job, maneuvering the corporate ladder. But Olga, at eighty, recognizes value in her work, purely for the sake of the work itself. She's steadily making a slow, quiet contribution to others' well-being. Some might consider Olga's effort insignificant. However, day after day, for decades, Olga serves others. Where would our world be without the Olgas who faithfully contribute in these countless ways?

THE WORK OF INVESTING

After reorienting to the truth that work is itself *good*, we need to tug at the thread a little further, digging into how investing is *work*. Many of us think of investing as this mysterious, passive endeavor, something handled by the experts far away in high-rise offices who yell into their headsets all day and punch numbers on keyboards that make companies, economies, and 401(k)s rise and fall. Many of us assume the professionals out there somehow pull all the strings while we're inactive bystanders as the machines roll on.

Or we may think of investing as gambling or speculating, playing the stock market as if we're pulling the lever on a slot machine or picking numbers for the next Mega Millions. One survey[13] discovered how over half of Americans consider investing on par with buying tickets at the dog tracks. Warren Buffet, one of our most respected investing titans, chastised[14] the market's high stakes, get-rich-quick culture for operating like a "gambling parlor." In an annual letter written to Berkshire Hathaway investors, he insisted that purchasing a stock for immediate profit is like flipping a coin. "Half of all coin-flippers will win their first toss; none of those winners has an expectation of profit if he continues to play the game."

Actual investing is not gambling; it is work we do with our money. Maybe some of us need to redefine investing. Let's take a stab:

Investing (verb)

1. to use our resources to purchase a portion (usually a very tiny portion, often through a mutual fund or ETF)

of some company an investor believes in and wants to help succeed

2. to become an owner of a business

Investing puts our money to *work*. Investing *works*. As in, investing puts our values and money to work by funding businesses. We, too, must work to invest well. Without research and intention, we aren't investing, we are gambling. Investing (well) is work (that is good).

There's a common misperception that investing is merely a mechanism for returns, meeting financial goals and weighing the risks involved. However, things change when we understand investing by the definition above—company ownership. As investors (owners) in these investment portfolios, we should be engaged (or *invested*) in everything about the companies in the portfolio: their purpose, their products, their services, their practices, their values, their risks, their impact, and their profit. As owners, we become ethically responsible for what the business does. We become partners who are making their endeavors possible. We hope to receive profits from the business, and so we're rooting for their success.

We align our values with almost every area of our lives—how we raise our children, how we vote, and the charitable causes we support. What if we did the same with our investments? When we understand investing as company ownership, this magnifies the need to apply our values.

What do you value? So many investment portfolios are problematic because these portfolios are disconnected from ownership and only focused on returns. We become owners of companies we don't believe in, making money from products or services that harm God's image bearers and diminish the beauty and goodness of His world. Too many investments exploit people rather than serve them. Too many investments make the world worse, not better. And as owners, too often we find ourselves profiting from the very things we want to resist.

Proverbs 1:10–19 levels a stern warning against receiving profit from evil enterprises or from the suffering of others, calling such profit "ill-gotten gain." An astounding number of businesses profit from harming rather than helping their customers (tobacco, subprime lending, abortion, pornography, online gambling, and many more). And many people don't realize that their investment portfolios may very well include businesses like these.

It's uncomfortable to recognize how as owners in these companies, we profit from "ill-gotten gain." We profit from harm done to others. Businesses should aim to serve the common good, and as owners, we have the responsibility to see that our businesses fulfill their purpose. As an owner, then, our first question is not how much money will I make but what kind of companies and businesses do I want to own?

We do want to profit from business, absolutely. Profit is necessary for a business to be sustainable. We must have profit to reinvest back into the business if we are going to expand its purpose to contribute to the common good. It's right for profit to be shared with the investors who took the risk to fund the business. And it's right for profit to be shared with the poor since business is an engine for wealth creation. In Deuteronomy, it was God who gave Israel the ability to create wealth (8:18). However, profit should never be the primary (and certainly not exclusive) goal. Profit is what happens when business is done well, when a business meets needs and serves the community.

What we need is an expansive view of profit that considers a wider frame. Our goal should be the common good, profit for the owners but also for the employees, for the customers, for the suppliers, for creation, and for the whole community. It should come as no surprise how (as Fred Reichheld argues in his excellent book *The Ultimate Question*) businesses that focus on their purpose and on creating compelling value for customers, employees, and other stakeholders are often the ones who also evidence sustainable profits and customer loyalty. A focus on the common good with an eye on profit is in fact how we generate the resources for more good work to get funded, for families to have what they need to be healthy and stable, and for communities to gain access to all that they need to thrive. The concern is not profit itself but whether our profit serves the common good or simply rips away resources for the benefit of only a few.

This is why business, in addition to the necessary work that nonprofits and governments provide, plays a unique role. Businesses, at their best, operate as an engine, creating new wealth and opportunities. They create value for their owners but also for all their stakeholders (owners, absolutely, but employees, customers, and everyone they touch).

Business either creates value in the world or extracts value (and some do a mix of both, which is what makes these decisions complicated at times). A business that's fulfilling its deep purpose, though, adds value, making a community or just life better, or perhaps addresses some human need. A healthy business always imagines and works to create a future where everyone can profit. This is why the vision we're casting for investing is so big. Investing like this *works*.

On the other hand, businesses that measure success only by looking at short-term stock prices or short-term profits for owners tend to make decisions that are not in the best interest of the long-term health of the business. A selfish, short-sighted vision inevitably leads to extracting resources without considering the monumental costs that will endure long past the next SEC filing. In the same Deuteronomy passage where God told Israel that He had enabled them to build wealth, God further explained Israel's obligations. God insisted on certain priorities Israel must remember as they managed this wealth God entrusted to them: They must take care of the poor, the alien, and the sojourner. What we do with our money—it should never be just for ourselves. The investments we make with our money are part of how we participate in the common good, caring for all our neighbors.

One of the ways investing works for the common good is by allowing us to move our money to relieve areas of deep pain. Sherrie Smith, a former colleague of mine, had a clear moment when this vision solidified for her. "I remember when my role as a values-based investor became most personal to me," she explained. "I have a niece with type-I diabetes, and my brother and his wife are up many nights just trying to make sure their daughter stays alive." One day she realized that one of the companies she was investing in was working to create a bionic pancreas, a device that would manage the blood sugar and remove the constant threat that makes ordinary life so exhausting and terrifying. With this device, her family could sleep easily through the night. Her niece could spend the night with friends or a weekend with grandparents. "These moments clarify for me why I believe in this vision of business being for the good of humanity," she said. "I want to invest in companies that have this kind of positive impact on the world." She realized she wanted to invest in, to own and support, businesses that create, rather than extract, value. Who wouldn't want to be a part of companies like this?

As we move into this expansive, compelling vision for how investing can do meaningful work, the questions crystalize. What kind of businesses and enterprises do we want to own, partner with, and help advance? How can we join God in making the whole world beautiful and good? How can we invest in a way that brings about human flourishing, wholeness, and justice? How can we respond to God's invitation to work out from Eden?

Investing Our Lives for the World's Joy

What kind of businesses and enterprises do you want to own and partner with in your investment portfolio? What kinds of business do you want to advance through your work? How can you join God in making the whole world beautiful? How can you work and invest in ways that bring human flourishing, wholeness, and justice? How can you respond to God's invitation to work out from Eden?

This Better World   3

Businesses You'd Be Proud to Own

> *Being good is good business.*
> Anita Roddick

My good friend Harry Pearson from Birmingham spent twelve years building a successful financial advisor practice. Aligning his faith into his work was important for Harry, and like most financial advisors, Harry integrated principles of generosity and contentment into client conversations. His approach to investing was only to maximize risk-adjusted returns to spur generosity.

It was a talk by Eventide's founding member Jason Myhre that had a profound impact on Harry. There were seventeen mugshots on the slide, and Jason said, "This was an escort service that was busted for prostitution in New York, called High Class New York." He hit a button and fifteen mugshots went away, leaving just two mugshots. He said, "These are the two guys that put up the money to start this business. They never worked a day in the business. They never made any money in the business except for being paid interest back on what they'd invested. All the other people were arrested and had jail time, but what do you think happened to these two guys?" Harry literally had no idea. Jason said, "Well, they were indicted alongside everyone else. But the question I want you to think about is this. If an earthly judge will find these two passive investors guilty of how they invested their money, how will your Heavenly Father find you on how you've invested His?"

Harry told me, "I remember that moment. The Lord got my attention. This became a question of who is the owner? If we believe that God is the owner of all things, then that makes us the steward of His things. If we're the steward of His things, shouldn't we consider aligning His assets with His principles and with companies that bless humankind instead of causing harm? That single moment changed me personally, my family personally. It changed the direction of our business and how we serve families. I had no idea what was going to take place from that moment."

As he reflected, Harry pieced together a framework that allowed his clients to find congruence. Conversations with his clients now begin with some version of this question:[15]

"What values do you have that you'd never want to violate just to make a profit?"

It's a powerful, clarifying question. And there's an accompanying question that's just as illuminating: What hopes do you have for the world that are so important to you that you want to use your resources to see them become a reality?

These are essential questions for investors. What kind of businesses do we want to own? What businesses do we want to partner with because we believe they add value and do good rather than extracting value and inflicting harm? These are the pressing questions each of us grapple with as soon as we begin to understand investing as ownership.

Unfortunately, this is the fundamental axiom investors easily forget: Investing is ownership. When we invest in a company, either directly or through a mutual fund purchasing shares on our behalf, we own portions of that business.

In the 1920s, Edward Leffle, an aluminum pot and pan salesman, launched the first modern open-end mutual fund, and the convenience of outsourcing investments to professionals made it remarkably easy to entrust money to portfolio managers who do not share the investor's values. Over the decades as fund holdings became less transparent, investors became increasingly disconnected from their businesses.

In the 1970s, a novel framework for risk management emerged, one fixating only on diversification. This myopic focus was concerned only with purchasing "the market" broadly rather than owning specific businesses that create goods and services to solve customers' problems and build cultures where employees thrive and advance. This radical paradigm upheaval inherently alienated investors from their companies. The new approach disconnected us from the fact that we own bits of these businesses and how we are responsible, as owners, for these companies. Broad, unfocused diversification led to investors owning a vast array of companies simply because they were part of some index (like the S&P 500), which necessarily includes owning all kinds of bad businesses with bad profit. Bad companies doing destructive things may have an abundant balance sheet, but can we really call money made through exploitation and injustice profit? Bad profits destroy value rather than create value.

If we're just buying "the market," we make no distinction between our capital going into a business promoting family and community renewal or our capital going into a business promoting addiction and environmental destruction. In the broad "market" scheme, diversification and reducing volatility are the only commitment. But for investors driven by our values, we carry much deeper, life-and-death concerns.

The purpose of investing is to provide capital to businesses creating goods that are actually *good* for the world and services that actually *serve* the world's needs.

However, when we shift the emphasis to investing in a nebulous market via a sophisticated, opaque mechanism, we forget this purpose. We forget why we're investing in the first place.

Seeing this wider reality of ownership (avoiding bad businesses and helping good businesses) was an important chapter in our founding. Early on, we thought mostly in terms of how businesses should be honest and how we should steer clear of ethical quandaries (profiting from vices, etc.). As we pondered the Genesis story, however, and stayed attuned to our hopes for the impact investments could make, our thinking transformed into much more holistic, creative possibilities.

On July 1, 2008, we launched our first product. We named it *Gilead* because in Scripture *Gilead* means "mountain of witness" or "hill of testimony." Gilead was the place where God did what seemed impossible. God used Gideon and only a few hundred soldiers to rescue Israel from the powerful, overpowering Midianite army. The Bible also refers to the "balm of Gilead," a potent medicinal salve. Our hope was that we would be part of something far larger than just our fledgling company. We hoped to be part of this "mountain of witness," a movement of people who, though perhaps it would only be a handful of us at first, might join God's call to be a healing remedy amid a suffering world.

We hoped that we could be part of reimagining how our investments catalyze significant, lasting change.

"We created Eventide to open up a space in investment management where real discernment takes place around ownership and the common good," Finny said, "and to make a way to invest in companies that create value." We wanted to invest in companies that we would be proud to invest in and proud to support. We wanted to invest in companies that met our clients' needs, helped others, and advanced good in the world.

This movement was barely a dribble. No one noticed. There wasn't so much as a whisper on Wall Street. No one knew or cared what we were doing. But we were invigorated, not only with the entrepreneurial rush, but also far more with this new fire that had been lit, this capacious, hopeful vision for how investments could create and sustain businesses doing good, necessary work. Every conversation pushed us to reckon with this fundamental starting point: What makes a good business? What kinds of businesses do we want to help succeed? What businesses would we be proud to own?

We absolutely wanted to own companies that we believed held a competitive edge and anticipated making stellar returns. This element was indispensable. However, this answer wasn't good enough. Every investment company aims for this, but we carried far bigger hopes. We wanted to help our clients invest with integrity by building portfolios that pursue this better world we're all longing to see. But what investments—what businesses—help bring about this better world?

What kind of businesses contribute to flourishing? What kind of businesses are good for the world? Whatever businesses those are, those are the ones we are looking for. Those are the businesses that galvanize and invigorate us.

The reality is that when my mind returns to Kerala and to Ammachi, these questions focus for me. It all becomes simpler and more intuitive. When I'm considering an investment, I'll sometimes wonder if Ammachi would smile. Could this help to make the kind of world that Ammachi would have called *good*?

Still, we need more comprehensive guidelines than this, ideals that help us describe what a business that's good for the world looks like. This framework is not just for me, Jason, and Finny or for the company we help to lead. My passion is for a societal shift that extends far beyond us. Anyone can do this good work, and each of us can do this work in our own way. To help us all, amid a sea of data and misinformation, to evaluate businesses that help to create a better world, we've identified five essential values, five ideals that guide us.

At their core, these ideals all emerge from our fundamental obligation: to honor God by loving our neighbors (a primary motivation underlying all we do and a central theme we'll return to in a later chapter to explore more in depth). Each of these ideals concretely expresses our conviction that good business loves its neighbors by creating value for rather than exploiting others. So, recognizing that as investors, we are owners and participants, these are the five values we look for in any business before we support them with our dollars. These markers point us to businesses that we don't have to apologize for or go to bed at night feeling guilty about how we're hurting others. These are businesses we'd be proud to own. I encourage you to consider your own values as you read and think about the types of businesses you'd be proud to own.

1. Respecting the Value and Freedom of All People

When Finny and I began to concretely arrange the core building blocks for an investing philosophy, we determined that our approach to investing must be grounded in the belief that every human is created in the image of God with intrinsic dignity, value, and worth. Respect and care for every single person is a non-negotiable for us.

As Christians, one of the two central instructions Jesus gave us was to love our neighbor—and investing is not exempted from this command. Since every human is made in God's image, every human (regardless of color or ethnicity or class or gender or religion or political persuasion or age) carries immense goodness and significance (and this is before anyone brings any skill or other "value" to the equation). We must never view God's beautiful image bearers as merely numbers in a forecasting chart or data points on an economic profile. People are more than consumers of goods, more than producers of products, more than bits to the machine.

It's remarkable, though, how quickly such a basic ideal gets trampled by corporate-speak. It's astounding how many workers in so many parts of the world labor under oppressive, dehumanizing conditions—sweat shops, inhumane hours, and scandalous pay far below a bare living wage. With each of these, it's a person with a face and a name and a family who's trying to claw their way into a better life. It's shocking how often, even now, people are denied opportunities to advance because of their ethnicity, gender, or religion. We might think this is a problem in remote parts of the world, all of it disconnected from American or Western companies. However, given our global economy and the interrelated reality of international business, these disturbing realities are often (like my experience in Pune) wedded to the companies most familiar to us.

Some of my passion around this, I know, grows from my story as an immigrant and how I have always felt like an outsider and sort of an outcast as a kid. I grew up as a Christian in a predominantly Hindu country, so often I found myself not going along with a lot of the prevailing assumptions. After arriving in the US, my family settled in Medford, Massachusetts, in an Irish and Italian neighborhood with one Indian family now tossed into the melting pot.

My classmates christened Sony and me with nicknames: Apu (the Indian character from *The Simpsons*) and Habib (from *Married . . . with Children*). They would follow us around, asking if our dad worked at the Kwik-E-Mart or the 7-Eleven. The worst harassers were two brothers, Tommy and James, who lived a couple of blocks away and made our daily walk to the bus stop like a march to the guillotine. One afternoon as I exited the bus, one of the boys gave me a fierce shove, sending me sprawling onto the gravel. Tommy and James jumped on me, driving their fists into my ribs. I gasped for air and tried desperately to catch sight of the bus driver, but through the flurry of fists, I only caught flashes of yellow pulling away. A crowd of kids circled, watching the Indian boy get pummeled. Mercifully, a mom ran off her porch and grabbed both boys by the collar.

Our neighbor Joe Platti, a retired Italian marine sergeant with lots of stories and an unlit cigar always hanging out of his mouth, took me under his wing. Joe taught me how to throw a mean right hook with an elbow follow-through that would shatter a jaw or nose. Joe installed a basketball hoop for Sony and me to come over and use, and he built us our first bikes. I began to love Joe as though he was my own grandfather; his wife Irene baked my first ever birthday cake on my tenth birthday. I'm grateful for Joe. Even while I was an outsider as a very young boy trying to get through elementary school, Joe made me feel like I belonged.

But at school, I knew I didn't belong. They stuck me in an ESL class with no instruction and just handed me a copy of *Tuck Everlasting*. I stared at the pages for hours and only saw hieroglyphics. I had a pink ticket for the cafeteria, which meant I was a free-lunch kid. I thought I'd arrived the day they handed me a blue ticket moving me up the economic ladder to a reduced-price lunch and required me to shell out 40¢ for my corn dog, peas, and fruit Jell-O.

We lived on the first floor of a three-story/three-family house. On our floor, five of us shared two bedrooms, with my sister Julie, Sony, and I crammed into the bedroom right next to the kitchen. I didn't realize that I arrived at school every day smelling like curry, cumin, and garlic, but I saw the curled noses and grossed-out expressions. I heard the jokes.

I'm guessing that a lot of us, in one way or another, know something about what it feels like to be the outsider, and seeing others at the margins, most of us want to help. When we're at our best, our heart responds to those who are vulnerable. However, some of us need help connecting the dots between our convictions and our investments, especially when those investments seem like just numbers on a screen. The challenge is to allow our best instincts (to protect and value life) to animate our investing choices. If we want to be part of making a better world, then our core values and hopes must influence our investments.

Here's the baseline we look for in any company before we consider partnering with them: They must value each person's freedom to live a good, meaningful life. We want to support businesses that consider those whom society often forgets and those who might not normally factor into a company's business model. This requires taking a hard look at a company's workers and surrounding community. Where are the blind spots? (And to be sure, we have blind spots too.) Who is being forgotten? This value explains some of why we're so keen on investing in companies researching cures for orphan diseases, those rare maladies that affect a tiny percentage of people and often receive little attention or funding. If there's a need that's being overlooked and it's a need that we can meet, it's a thrill and joy to be part of the solution.

This value also means we resist any industry that takes advantage of the poor and the marginalized. We expect the companies we own to guard our most precious gift— human life—in every way and at every stage, whether in the womb or in an underserved school, on a manufacturing line in Detroit or in the Philippines, or in accessible healthcare options for the young and for aged bodies nearing their final breaths. We refuse to profit from business that subverts human freedom by preying on people's addictive and destructive behaviors such as gambling, pornography, tobacco, and alcohol. Human life and freedom are our most basic rights and gifts, and it's our fundamental expectation for any business we support.

Every person. Every life. Each overflowing with abundant dignity and worth. This is where we start. The rest of our investing values flow from here and merely extend this commitment to value and protect life. *All* life.

2. Demonstrating a Concern for Justice and Peace

Secondly, we look for businesses that demonstrate a concern for justice and peace. We want to further businesses that actively pursue fair, ethical relationships with their customers, suppliers, and business partners—and businesses that avoid products and services that promote weapons production and proliferation. It's very difficult to love your neighbor if you're not being fair with them. It's even more difficult to love your neighbor if you're helping to kill them.

Do businesses understand that they are not bystanders but key players in shaping how workers earn a living wage and how we resist discrimination and racism? Do corporations understand that they are part of the neighborhoods and the economies and social fabric where they are located—and that this should have significant bearing on the decisions they make? To be clear, I am not advocating for businesses to avoid their core purpose to pursue culture wars or political agendas. Rather, I believe that a business should be and do good and that the products, services, and management practices from good businesses will pursue justice.

Jaunita and I lived in Dallas, Texas, for ten years, where I became involved with a ministry that serves South Dallas communities. There is an immense disparity of wealth between North and South Dallas, with the southern portion of the city suffering from food injustice. Between 35 and 40 percent of the residents in five South Dallas zip codes live below the poverty line, and much of the area is considered a food desert.[16] Because grocers prefer to place their stores in the more affluent communities that yield higher margins, many people have no access to healthy groceries within a ten-mile radius. Because many South Dallas residents don't have easy access to transportation, they often are left to buy unhealthy and more expensive food at convenient stores and even liquor stores.

The City of Dallas once offered $3 million to any grocer who would open a grocery store providing "fresh produce and healthy food" in the "southern Dallas food desert."[17] Not a single grocer responded. I used to wonder why grocers like Whole Foods Market have not opened a store in South Dallas. Most of South Dallas residents are African American, and the Whole Foods Market webpage in July 2020 proclaimed in large, bold lettering: "Racism has no place here." Amazon, the parent company of Whole Foods, has donated over $10 million to organizations connected to the Black Lives Matter movement and for a season matched employees' donations to organizations like the Equal Justice Initiative, NAACP, and the Black Lives Matter Foundation. However, wouldn't the most obvious and impactful way for a grocery store to fight racial injustice towards the African American community be to make their products and services available to those in the community who most need them?

Justice and peace require action. This is work that we must do. It's not enough for us to merely find companies who aren't engaged in overtly bad practices. Rather, we want to join up with businesses who understand the larger picture that they are responsible actors and can play a massive role in advocating for—and enacting—justice and peace. We want to support businesses who have, intertwined in their mission as members of the economic and social community, a meaningful, persistent concern for peace and justice.

3. Promoting Family and Community

A third crucial value we look for in a business is how they promote family and community. This is another ideal that resonates with my story. When I think about Kerala's immense impact on me (and specifically my home village of Kangazha), it's all connected to how that place submerged me within the deep, nurturing waters of family and a nourishing, interconnected community.

In Kerala, our family lived, ate, and laughed together in one intergenerational house. We had an outhouse for the bathroom, which posed a difficulty at night because there were snakes in the surrounding forest. At night, Sony and I would pee out the back door. You couldn't pay us to walk through the thicket to the outhouse with King Cobras stalking us through the dark. And have I mentioned the heat—that thick, sticky, sweet heat as if someone drizzled syrup over the blistering air? A single electric line drooped toward our house, wrapping around a metal pipe jutting out above a window. Most every night, the power cut off. Every evening, I watched forlorn as the fan slowed, the blades winding down to a full stop. I imagine it's how a man in a dank dungeon would feel as he watched the final flicker of light disappear from the candle.

Sony and I shared a room with our grandparents. We brothers shared a bed with Appacha, while Ammachi slept on a twin against the opposite wall. The suffocating humidity and Sony and Appacha snoozing and pumping heat—have you ever tried to sleep next to two snoring ovens? When I couldn't stand it anymore, I climbed down, brushed away the coconut beetles that looked like miniature rhinos, flattened my body onto the floor, and turned my head sideways so I could press as much flesh as possible against the cool concrete.

It was awful. And it was beautiful. While I'd never want to go back to a world without air conditioning, I'd give anything for my children to feel what I felt surrounded by such love and such a natural sense of stability, protection, and belonging. This ingrained stability and belonging was not simply because of my family living under one roof but was rather connected to how our family was immersed in a vibrant web of community. These deep and wide relationships welcomed us and nurtured us, a social fabric that existed long before us and would exist long after us.

Indian novelist Arundhati Roy says that the stories that shape us are like an old house at night where our ancestors are still whispering inside. This is true for me. I often walked with Appacha to the village, Kangazha, where he'd purchase vegetables, rice, and fish at the market. He bought me rock candy or puff pastries stuffed with ground beef and masala for three rupees each. The trips would take forever because neighbors would wave to us, and we'd inevitably stop to talk. If anyone had a need, we felt responsible to do our best to help. Whenever Sony or I would roam, someone in the neighborhood would have an eye on us. We all watched out for each other. We belonged to one another. That sense of safety and attachment formed me in the deepest ways. It was a community that still feels like my home. Even now, I still hear the whispers.

I don't want to make Kerala sound idyllic. Like any place, there was abuse and selfishness. Women didn't have the same opportunities and freedoms as men. And there was certainly an intolerable disparity between the rich and the poor. My family lived right at the poverty line. We had enough but just barely. There were so many others far poorer than us who lived at the jagged edge of survival. I remember knowing that I had one friend at school who was rich because every day he pulled this magnificent wonder from his lunchbox: a peanut butter and jelly sandwich on sliced white bread. My sweet Ammachi didn't know any better, so she told me it was called "beena butter." There was extensive classism, remnants of the caste system. Colonialism left a deep wound. The healthcare system was often abysmal. I can't describe the extent of the opportunities my family found when we moved to the States, and the hardships of so many back home grieve me even now.

Still, there was also much beauty and grace in Kerala. And one of the gifts that has shaped me the most is this mutual responsibility, woven into who we were, to guard family cohesion and to nurture healthy communities. We need more of this here now. We need to push against our excessive individualism and take responsibility to protect the most vulnerable among us: our children.

Protection at this level requires collective commitment and action. While some corporations may view children merely as consumers, we want to support businesses that see our children as our most precious gifts whom we are entrusted to protect. For me, it also means resisting industries that target children and adolescents (for example: violent entertainment, pornography, and the tobacco industry). At Eventide, we have never in our history ever invested in any of the social media companies because we have always had concerns that social media erodes family and community.

Building thriving communities also requires supporting low-income communities that have too often been exploited or abandoned to fend for themselves. Rather than allowing struggling neighborhoods' resources to be drained away in service to the ravenous demands of a voracious economy, we look for businesses who recognize that for long-term flourishing every neighborhood and every community is essential for the common good. Whenever any community fails to thrive, this is a burden we all must bear and seek to remedy. A healthy business, like a healthy economy, lifts everyone. A diseased business, like a diseased economy, raises some while pushing down others.

We aim to encourage healthy businesses. We want to join with businesses that promote families and communities rather than tear them down.

4. Exhibiting Responsible Management Practices

When searching for good companies, the fourth marker we look for is responsible management practices. We want to partner with businesses that are led, top to bottom, with integrity. We want to support companies who demonstrate intentional leadership that is proactively seeking fair dealing with their employees, their communities, their suppliers, their customers, and yes—their competitors. What is their work environment? Are employees treated well? Do they have a history of playing loose with regulations and safety practices? We pore over the company's product history to see if the products they create or the services they offer improve people's lives. We're looking for businesses led by people who do what they say rather than publishing corporate-speak that sounds enlightening and offers good PR while covering greed, dishonesty, or malfeasance.

In 2010, the tragedy at Foxconn's Longhua plant in China made global headlines. This mammoth, sprawling city-sized plant manufactured the iPhone by the millions. However, in 2010, workers began throwing themselves off the roofs of buildings in desperate acts of suicide. That year, there were eighteen suicide attempts, fourteen deaths, and another twenty workers who were talked off the ledge. The situation grew so dire that Foxconn hung large nets from buildings to catch bodies. A *Guardian* article describes the grim reality: "Suicide notes and survivors told of immense stress, long workdays and harsh managers who were prone to humiliate workers for mistakes, of unfair fines and unkept promises of benefits."[18]

This was absolutely a failure of leadership. A systemic, inhumane culture pervaded, but so long as the iPhones rolled off the assembly line and profits accelerated, managers and those in the boardroom didn't see a problem. "It's not a good place for human beings," said Xu, one former worker. The conditions were cruel, and workers had no recourse. There were so many Chinese looking for jobs, and management knew that if someone caused problems, they could simply fire them and hire the next person in line.

When your only goal is short-term profit, it reveals poor leadership and encourages bad practices. How can you encourage an expansive vision for the common good when the anxiety and pressure of immediate profit is treated as the only serious concern? Business strategist Fred Reichheld put a fine point here: "It is difficult to get a man to understand something when his salary depends upon his not understanding it."[19]

Of course, such callous leadership and short-sighted vision will eventually level a severe cost. I believe the best companies (thus the best investments) are those who have a long view and who build a sustainable culture, offering meaningful work to employees as well as products that offer something of genuine value to their customers. As Mihaly Csikszentmihalyi reminds us, a business is successful to the extent that it provides a product or service that contributes to happiness in all of its forms.[20] It is remarkable how many of these five values we're exploring are ignored by investors when, in addition to being better for society, they can actually lead us to healthier companies that make better long-term investments. There's a lot of common-sense wisdom here if we would just listen to it.

Supporting responsible management practices is a good investment principle, but it's also a deeply spiritual principle. God has a lot to say about this. In words that land like thunder, God announces how He will come in judgement against "those who exploit workers."[21] And for any of us who profess faith, the words from Isaiah, one of Israel's prophets, ought to make us sit up straight. God expressed his displeasure with the people's acts of piety, their public displays of fasting and prayer, because while they were living their "spiritual lives," they were "exploit[ing] all [their] workers."[22] James warns of how "all the workers [we've] exploited and cheated cry out for judgement."[23]

Many years ago, Sony shared with me an often-overlooked story from 2 Samuel 23. While David and his soldiers were locked in a deadly conflict with the Philistines, David expressed his longing to taste the refreshing water once again from the well in Bethlehem. However, Bethlehem was the Philistines' stronghold. Undaunted and under the cover of night, three of David's warriors snuck across enemy lines, stole into the enemy garrison, and returned with a fresh flask of cool water. When David realized what his warriors had done, he refused to drink the water, pouring it out onto the ground instead. His refusal was not ingratitude but rather his horror over the realization of how his poor leadership had put his warriors in danger. David could not drink. There was, as my brother Sony put it, "blood in the water."

While David was horrified over what he'd done and refused to enjoy the spoils of the ill-advised raid, many corporate boardrooms would have cheered him on and offered him a bonus. Business leaders who risk the lives and well-being of others in the pursuit of profit are often rewarded with big offices and a promotion. This is the leadership ethos I want to resist.

Instead, we're on the hunt for businesses that are led well with honesty and integrity. We seek business leaders who are proactively trustworthy and fair to their employees and to everyone they engage, leaders who know that the people who work for them as well as the people whom they serve are their first responsibility. We're looking for those companies who take pride in their work and who create products or services that provide something helpful and meaningful to their customers.

5. Practicing Environmental Stewardship

Finally, we're searching for companies that practice environmental stewardship. We want to find businesses who recognize that our land and water and air are immense gifts to us that we must nurture and protect. This value returns us to the Genesis story and the call God gave humans to move out of Eden and make the world fruitful. We are caretakers, not simply consumers.

For too long, we've viewed this earth God has entrusted to our care as an infinite source of unlimited supply, allowing us to devour it with our insatiable appetites. Some even misunderstand the Genesis call for humans to "subdue" the earth as carte blanche permission for us to use creation however we like. However, God did not commission us to dominate or harm creation, nor master Earth's creatures like an abusive circus trainer. Rather, God invited us to make His work our work. As we discussed earlier, He created us in His image so that we can reflect God's image in our work. And God's creative work is always generative and good not extractive. Healthy work (thus healthy business), rather than sapping life or exploiting resources from a languishing community, instead ignites fresh possibilities, relieves suffering, nurtures wholeness amid decay, and suffuses beauty into barren, desolate spaces. Healthy businesses serve the common good, making the neighborhood better, the ecosystem better, and the future better— for everyone.[24]

But in the old, unhealthy frame of mind, businesses are rarely asked to consider whether their practices or products hinder or help God's intentions for us to watch over His world. Nor are they required to factor in the actual cost of their business, the cost to the ground, water, and sky that they are using. We can no longer make this mistake.

The same Proverb that warns us against "ill-gotten gain" also describes the taking of profit unjustly from others as "plunder."[25] And when we extract the earth's resources with little thought for how we are robbing future generations (or robbing the poor now, the ones who always suffer the most from our negligence) of vital necessities—we plunder. We plunder the earth. And plundering is the exact opposite of being a steward and caretaker.

When I'm back in India riding in an autorickshaw, I'll often see workers doing road repairs. Elderly women, each of them someone's Ammachi, hunch over rusted metal barrels, burning old tires until they melt into thick liquid. This is a horrific, filthy job, standing in the roasting heat stirring tar while inhaling black smoke deep into their lungs. The job pays pennies, and the only people they can get to do it are those who are too feeble to do anything else. These stooped, wizened women need to eat; they need to help their family eat. And so they endure the blazing rays and stir black death as it spills into the air and into their bodies. Long after we pass, their image lingers along with the stench of seared, smoldering rubber.

The truth is, though, that while in our advanced economies you'd see nothing like that out in the open, our foolishness goes on inside sophisticated boardrooms and out in fields with expensive machines and toxic chemicals. The fact is that the wealthiest, largest nations have made the bulk of our environmental mess always at the expense of the poorest nations and our poorest neighbors. As Peter Harris, the founder of Christian conservation ministry A Rocha, often says, "The poor live downstream and downwind."[26]

When I speak about the air, water, and land pollution in India, I don't think that my American friends understand just how bad it is. It is so bad that, a few years ago, the daughter of a family friend from Boston died from an asthma attack when visiting New Delhi. Often in India, I've seen small, grimy pools, the only source of water for the poor in the village. In that same water, you'll have children drinking, dogs and cows bathing, and people washing their clothes and dishes. (I've even seen people washing their bikes and an autorickshaw.) The wealthy would never drink this water. They have purifying systems, private wells, and easy access to bottled water. When mining or industrial pollution goes unchecked, it is always the poor who pay the price. The poor live near the factories. It's the poor whose food gets contaminated, and the poor who breathe the suffocating air while walking and riding their bicycles and motorcycles.

When we refuse to tend to creation, people suffer, but when we steward the environment, it's one tangible way that we care for the poor. Further, caring for the environment is a way we love our children and our children's children.

When I was a boy, the forest was my home. I still breathe deepest when I'm among the trees or near a river. Eventide sponsored the planting of four thousand trees, and I can't tell you the joy I felt when I saw the pictures of those saplings in the ground. Whenever I take my family back to Kerala, I grieve that my children won't encounter elephants the way that was so commonplace for me. They won't see those sweet goliaths trudging down the village road with their trunks curled and tails swatting flies. In Kerala, we had an ingrained sense that we shared our home with all living creatures and growing things. You rarely see elephants in Kerala anymore, except within sanctuaries or the life-sized display of fifteen wax elephants decked out in gold pakhars in the lobby of the Kochi airport.

This beautiful world is ours to tend to and care for, and we need to protect it. God's vision inspires us to do more than curb the harm we inflict but to participate in the world's healing. "We have a critical role to play," says A Rocha Kenya's director Colin Jackson, "in ensuring that creation not just survives but thrives."[27] The prophet Isaiah tells us of God's intentions to "create new heavens and a new earth," a promise reiterated again in Revelation 21.[28] And this new, healed creation, Isaiah says, will fuel human gladness and joy. A good world instigates joy.

While Jesus will complete this ultimate healing in the future that He promises for us, we are called to join in this work now wherever we are and whatever work in which we are engaged. "Isaiah's invitation," wrote Tish Warren, "isn't to simply wait around for God to usher in a reborn world, but to participate in God's ongoing work of repair and renewal."[29] Warren described how this Christian vision of stewarding creation inspired the formation of the Royal Society for the Prevention of Cruelty to Animals, which led to outlawing bear-baiting where a bear was chained and forced to fight dogs, and to Ethiopia's "church forests" where Ethiopian Orthodox Tewahedo churches nurture and protect green oases in the midst of the barren desert.

We are to be part of the healing, and the good news is that remarkable companies are discovering revolutionary advancements towards environmental stewardship with manufacturing processes and technological solutions. They're learning how to help us be more sustainable in our use of resources, how to reduce environmental impact, and how to live and work cleaner. We want to partner with and support these companies who are leading us into these new possibilities. Can you imagine the joy we'll find in being part of the solution, part of God's long intention to make the world whole?

If you're going to own a business, isn't a company pursuing these five values the kind of business you'd want to own? What other values would you add? Take some time to write down the values that matter most to you in the businesses you'd want to own.

If you have a financial advisor, ask them to provide you with a list of the top ten or twenty companies in your portfolio along with a description of the product that the company produces. Consider if that product is genuinely good for the customer and society? This is the most basic place to start.

If you don't have a financial advisor but have a 401(k) plan, it can be harder because the 401(k) plan will often show only the names of the target date funds you are invested in. The industry has made it really hard for the average person to see the problems. You'll need to do the hard but worthwhile work of understanding which mutual funds and ETFs the target date fund is invested in and then look at the top holdings of each underlying mutual fund and ETF.

No company will embody all these values perfectly. And no investment company will either. However, if we're going to be part of making this better world, then it will mean making choices that actively move us in this direction, taking concrete steps toward a future that requires more than platitudes.

This vision of God's better world compels us to spurn harmful, oppressive practices and embrace a healthy, flourishing horizon. Together, we can invest in this better world.

Investing Our Lives for the World's Joy

What values do you hold so strongly that you'd never violate them just to make a profit? What hopes for the world do you consider so important that you'd expend your resources to help them become a reality? Take time to write them down.

Loving Neighbors   **4**

Investing to Practice the Great Commandment

> *The gospel at its best deals with the whole man, not only his soul but his body, not only his spiritual well-being, but his material well being. Any religion that professes to be concerned about the souls of men and is not concerned about the slums that damn them, the economic conditions that strangle them and the social conditions that cripple them is a spiritually moribund religion awaiting burial.*
>
> Martin Luther King, Jr.

We are responsible for our neighbors. Perhaps this is the single thread running through all the ideas we've explored. Everything I'm saying circles round this one clarifying principle. If we are genuinely watching out for our neighbors, we will instinctively resist any investment that perpetrates harm (what, in the next chapter, I'll call fighting dragons), and we'll naturally search out those investments that promote whatever serves the common good (what I'll call tending gardens). The call to love our neighbor—this really is the start and the end.

Regardless of one's religious or philosophical viewpoint, for most of human history some version of the ancient axiom we know as the Golden Rule has outlined a basic, fundamental responsibility to treat those around us with care and dignity. For Christians, the call to love our neighbor pulses at the core of the uncomplicated (though never *easy*) vision defining how we are to live. When one of Israel's religious leaders asked Jesus to name the greatest commandment that humans are to follow, He answered with clarity: "You shall love the Lord your God with all your heart and with all your soul and with all your strength and with all your mind, and your neighbor as yourself."[30] Later, one of Jesus' disciples summed up our obligation succinctly: "the entire law is fulfilled in keeping this one command: 'Love your neighbor as yourself.'"[31] Love God. Love neighbors. These are the basics.

However, the religious leader (whom the Bible tells us is also a lawyer) was apparently rattled by the implications of this unequivocal command, and he began to quibble over the fine print. "But who is my neighbor?" he asked. "Name the people—exactly—that you're saying I'm responsible to love." It sounds like a fellow looking for loopholes.

Rather than answer directly, Jesus told a tale about a Jewish man traveling on the road from Jerusalem to Jericho who had the bad fortune of running into a gang of hoodlums. The roving thugs beat the poor fellow, stripped him bare, stole everything he had, tossed him into the ditch, and left him for dead. Eventually, another traveler walked his way, a priest of all things, a holy man. This is precisely the right kind of person you hope will happen on the scene when you're in trouble, right? Maybe not. The man writhing in the ditch must have cried out in joyous relief that help was near, but the priest darted to the other side of the road and hurried past. A Levite happened by next, another holy man, but he does the exact same thing—looks away and scoots by as fast as he can.

Finally, a Samaritan appeared on the horizon. Here the story takes a shocking turn. Samaritans were (as far as the Jews were concerned) exactly the *wrong* kind of person. According to common prejudice, Samaritans were reviled for being multiracial, political traitors, and long-loathed enemies. But the Samaritan stops. He bandages the wounds, lifts the broken man onto his own donkey, and carries him to the closest town. There the Samaritan finds an inn and—can you believe it—pays all the expenses so the wounded traveler can recover.

The religious lawyer must have stood there, mouth agape, at the story's close.

"What do you think?" Jesus asked. "Which of the three became a neighbor to the man attacked by robbers?"

I imagine the lawyer fumbling for words then offering the only possible reply: "The one who treated him kindly."

"Go and do the same," Jesus said.[32]

Jesus invited the lawyer, and all of us, to follow the Samaritan's example to resist the temptation to look past a stranger's need and instead pause and care for anyone who's abandoned, anguished, or beaten down by injustice.

Something stirs deep inside us whenever we hear this iconic story. It awakens our sense of how the world ought to be, how *we* ought to be, and explains at least in part why The Good Samaritan is one of Jesus' most-beloved parables. Though we're often trapped in our own small, selfish worlds, the deeper truth is that we ache for wrongs to be righted, for needs to be met, and wounds mended. We're infuriated when the priest and the Levite walk past, and we cheer when the Samaritan acts with compassion. Intuitively, when we hear Jesus' words, our heart tells us that that is right and that we are supposed to go and do the same.

Deep in our bones, we intuitively know that we are entrusted with the care of others, with our fellow humans. If we don't watch out for one another, then who do we think will? "Christ has no body now on earth but yours," wrote Teresa of Ávila in the sixteenth century. "No hands but yours, no feet but yours; yours are the eyes through which to look at Christ's compassion to the world, yours are the feet with which he is to go about doing good, and yours are the hands with which he is to bless us now."[33] Our feet. Our ears. Our eyes. Our work. Jesus entered the world in order to heal and bless, and Jesus uses us to do it.

NEIGHBORS ALL AROUND

Whenever I ponder these neighbor ideas, there's an echo deep in my soul. I've shared how in Kerala my family was interwoven into a wide community of friendship and belonging. We cared for one another and watched out for each other. If someone needed food or was sick, neighbors stepped in.

My parents and grandparents always found themselves stepping into the community's need, whatever the deficit happened to be. As a boy, whenever I looked out our window, I'd peer out over the cemetery with the cracked concrete mausoleum and rows of markers. The church needed land for a graveyard, and so my grandfather, poor as he was, donated his own backyard. Often, when I visit Kerala, I return to that plot and walk those rows of graves. Neighborliness ran deep for us, extending even to our dead.

However, when we moved to the US, for the first time I experienced what it was like to genuinely be an outsider. I told you about the shock I felt as my uncle drove us out of JFK and through the sensory overload of New York City, me in the back row of the van, mouth agape. I mentioned my uncle handing me a burger and my gag reflex. If this was the food I would be expected to eat, then I guess you could add starvation to my other worries. In Medford, you'll remember how we were the only Indian family in our neighborhood, and how I endured a steady barrage of jokes, snide jabs, and isolation.

On my first day of junior high, I sat next to the girl who would later win the vote, naming her the most beautiful girl in school, in our high school yearbook. And there she was, sitting next to me.

I wiped my sweaty palms on my jeans, and my mouth turned to cotton. My mind awhirl, I couldn't push out a single word. I don't think she'd ever met an Indian before, and I only sat there, looking straight ahead and trying to remember what day of the week it was.

She waved her hands at me with exaggeration and asked in a slow, over-pronounced cadence: "*Doooo . . . youuu . . . speeeaaakkk . . . Ennnnnggglllissshh?*" My face went as strawberry red as is possible for a brown-skinned boy. I'm sure she wasn't trying to be mean, but it was clear I didn't belong.

We all have our own stories of when we stood on the outside looking in. Maybe reconnecting to our stories is an essential part of answering the call to love our neighbors. Everyone needs a neighbor. Sometimes we're the neighbor in need. Sometimes we're the neighbor who meets the need.

NAMING THE NEIGHBORS

As we work together to reimagine what's possible, we discover a whole other universe of ways that investing in businesses enacts a robust, sustained, and active love for our neighbors. These possibilities ignite all my energy. But first, we find ourselves with the same question the religious lawyer put to Jesus. From our beginning, this single dilemma has dogged us: As investors, who are our neighbors?

I still remember, when we were first dreaming up Eventide, Jason Myhre's formative query. "If one of the greatest commandments is to love our neighbors," Jason asked, "then who are the neighbors that businesses are supposed to serve?" We pondered and read and eventually concluded that a business's neighbors encompass everyone who is impacted by and in any way intersects with the business. This is a massive, comprehensive circle—a whole lot of neighbors.

Dolores Bamford, our Co-Chief Investment Officer at Eventide, explains this without any ambiguity: "Your neighbors are all of the people who are affected by the products and operations of the companies you invest in." It's helpful to make this concrete and manageable by thinking of six specific neighbors or six groups of people we are responsible to consider as we invest. Here are neighbors every business has:

1. the employees who make the business run
2. the customers who use the products or services
3. the many companies and people who make up the supply chain, providing all the company needs to operate
4. the communities that host the business
5. the environment that sustains (or suffers from) the business
6. the broader society a company inhabits

Of course, this mosaic-of-neighbors idea flies in the face of so much of the investing and business world's bedrock assumptions. Milton Friedman, the Nobel Prize-winning economist, popularized the idea that a company's only concern was to its shareholders with zero social responsibilities to the wider community or the common good.[34] However, as we listened to Jesus, pondered stories like the Good Samaritan, and just paid attention to our own basic sense of right and wrong, we cemented our core conviction that companies absolutely do have neighbors, and as investors in those companies, we are responsible to love and work toward their good.

This means that when we're considering taking a stake in a company, the process is far more involved than merely rummaging through balance sheets and making sure the business isn't engaged in something we find objectionable. We dig deep. Remember, we're looking to own a portion of this business. We're looking to support this enterprise and join with them in what they are putting into the world. We want to own companies who take care of their neighbors. Do they pay their employees well, and do they foster a healthy culture? Do they serve customers or merely use them? Do they strive to create an ecosystem where their vendors and suppliers flourish? Do they think about their impact on their host community and on the natural resources they share? Do they add value by what they do? Are they contributing to the world becoming a better place?

I remember in Eventide's early days an awkward encounter I had at a wedding. A wealthy businessman, a friend of my extended family, was there with his entourage. Our Indian community had given him the nickname "Millionaire." Wherever he was, he always worked the room, always selling the next deal. He flaunted his expensive suits and flashy watches. At the wedding, one of Millionaire's associates cornered me. He had heard we were forming an investment firm grounded in our Christian values, and he had opinions. "You can't do that," he said, agitated. "You can't mix business and faith because in business, you have to cut corners—or you'll fail." He was spouting Millionaire's core philosophy.

After the short exchange, I stood there dumbfounded while the party swirled around me. I couldn't comprehend how anyone (especially those who said they took

Jesus seriously) could ever envision separating their work from their core values or basic human obligations. However, Millionaire didn't think his values had anything at all to do with his investments. Those were two worlds separated by an impenetrable wall. Millionaire didn't believe his businesses had any neighbors to whom he was responsible. His only responsibility was to himself to grow revenue. If he had to cut corners, if he had to hurt others, so be it. This was business. Being ruthless—that's a virtue. Loving others—that's weak and naïve. We could have explained to Millionaire how we identify our investment's neighbors, or we could have told Millionaire we were investing in time travel. Either would have been equally ludicrous to him. Roughly a year later, Millionaire was caught running a Ponzi scheme. My dad, along with many of Millionaire's longtime friends, even lost a chunk of money.

While few businesses run such outrageously dishonest schemes, it's common for businesses to completely fail to consider all their neighbors whenever they're mapping out their strategy and priorities. Instead, a myopic, shortsighted view on profit compels them to approach customers and employees as disposable commodities—while the rest of their neighbors barely even register.

In his monumental book *The Ultimate Question*, Fred Reichheld, a business strategist known as a leader in the "loyalty economics" school of thought, reveals the bleak reality:

> Too many managers have come to believe that increasing [profits and shareholder value] requires exploiting customer relationships. So they raise prices whenever they can. They cut back on services or product quality to save costs and boost margins. Instead of focusing on innovations to improve value for customers, they channel their creativity into finding new ways of extracting value from customers.
>
> In short, companies regard the people who buy from them as their adversaries, to be coerced, molded, or manipulated as the situation permits. The Golden Rule—treat others as you would like to be treated—is dismissed as irrelevant in a competitive world of hardball tactics. Customers are simply a means to an end—fuel for the furnace that forges superior profits. This view is utter nonsense. Companies that let themselves be brainwashed by such a philosophy are headed into a sinkhole of bad profits, where true growth is impossible.[35]

Remember the Foxconn story where working conditions were so horrendous and suicide attempts so constant that they put out nets to catch the people who'd jump? Maybe we're tempted to feel smug and think that these disturbing working conditions are only international problems, but the unsettling truth is that we have our own abusive practices in the US. Some companies are serial offenders, cited for safety violations and manipulative, fraudulent hiring practices. A few years ago, one large fast-food chain paid $26 million to California cashiers and cooks who claimed their employer improperly withheld pay by illegally abusing overtime, ignoring mandates for regular meal breaks, and failing to provide the required uniforms.[36] When you have an oppressive work culture, you've failed to see your employees as neighbors.

Opposing something so obvious as overt exploitation or forced labor ought to be easy (though even that evil often goes unchecked), but addressing enmeshed, layered injustices requires a much more comprehensive view. Moving past this unambiguous line, when you take a deeper look at a company's wider neighbors, you discover how far the exploitation goes (the environment, the supply chain, the economy, the local communities and families, and the political structure). We'll never discover how far a problem reaches if we aren't specifically looking and considering all the people a company impacts. We'll often do harm, and rarely do good if we don't insist that the businesses we own are responsible to consider the wellbeing of all their neighbors.

In stark contrast to the dehumanizing practices mentioned above, business writers Kevin and Jackie Freiberg offer a far more compelling vision: "What if you could build a company that is as human as the human beings in it? What if you could create a culture that inspires passionate people to come to work fully awake, fully engaged, firing on all cylinders because they know they are doing epic work?"[37] And what if you built a company that inspired and invigorated not only employees but everyone in its orbit?

There is a New England–based medical device maker that demonstrates this wonderfully, starting a local program to provide healthcare for homeless individuals. This effort has borne incredible fruit such as higher sobriety rates and fewer visits to the emergency room. The initiative begs an important question: What if more companies thought more about how they could use their influence, industry knowledge, and resources not just to turn a profit, but to bless and transform the lives of their neighbors? It is incredible to dream about the endless possibilities— deadly cycles broken, families reunited, mental health restored. Companies have such an incredible capacity for good, even in their own backyards. Considering our investment's neighbors—both positive and negative impacts—this commitment has fueled our engagement with numerous businesses.

GOOD NEIGHBORS AND GOOD BUSINESS

Loving our neighbors isn't only an ethical practice; it's a smart business practice too. Herb Kelleher (the long-time beloved CEO of Southwest Airlines who was known for his push to make his airline the best employer in the industry) held a straightforward philosophy. "Your employees come first," Kelleher insisted. "And if you treat your employees right, guess what? Then they treat your customers well, and that means your customers come back and your shareholders are happy."[38]

R. Edward Freeman, professor of Business Administration at the University of Virginia Darden School of Business, put this succinctly: "'Business ethics' shouldn't be an oxymoron; it should be two words that are redundant to each other. . . . Thinking about stakeholders is thinking about business. And thinking about stakeholders is thinking about ethics. It comes to the same thing.[39]

Ultimately, building a dynamic, profitable company and being a good, honorable company are not ideas in competition but rather forces that work in tandem. Contrary to the notion that profitability requires a cutthroat mentality where someone must lose so that someone else can win, good companies make it possible for everyone to flourish. When a company creates value for its stakeholders, it's also creating value for its shareholders. These efforts work in tandem. Truly good companies create a larger pie for everyone.

In his book *Grow the Pie: How Great Companies Deliver Both Purpose and Profit*, Dr. Alex Edmans, Professor of Finance at London Business School, demonstrated how the "Top 100 Best Companies to Work for in America" significantly outperformed the rest of the field by a wide margin.[40] Being good neighbors and building a good, profitable company—these are two inseparable aims.

Loving our neighbors sits at the heart of any genuine pursuit of a good and meaningful life. Loving our neighbors is more than an ethical principle we feel compelled to abide by or a moral instruction we are obliged to keep. Rather, loving our neighbors is elemental to what it means to be truly human and is basic to living a life that fulfills our deep purpose. Loving our neighbors in our work is exactly the mandate that God gave us when He created us in His image.

If we set out to truly love our neighbors, this commitment will reshape and reinvigorate every facet of the work we pursue and the life we seek. Everything gets reordered. As our love for our neighbors begins to animate all we do, we'll inevitably find ourselves reimagining from the ground up our investment goals and philosophy, what success looks like, as well as the strategies we use to get us—and our neighbors along with us—to a good and beautiful end.

Investing Our Lives for the World's Joy

Ponder all the stakeholders your everyday work touches. Are you proud of how your work honors them and supports their well-being? When you consider your investment portfolio, do the companies you own do good for these stakeholders? What values do these businesses promote through their products and their management practices? Do you feel good about what you see? Are you proud to own these businesses?

Fighting Dragons 5

Investing to Resist Injustice and Oppression

> *I am so tired of waiting,*
> *Aren't you,*
> *For the world to become good*
> *And beautiful and kind?*
> *Let us take a knife and cut the world in two—*
> *And see what worms are eating*
> *At the rind.*
>
> Langston Hughes, "Tired"

A gloomy pall and the stench of death hung over Hamburg, Germany, choking the city and bringing this mighty port to its knees.[41] Refuse from a Russian migrant who suffered from cholera drained into the Elbe River, contaminating the water supply. Within six weeks, ten thousand citizens died. To make the story even more infuriating and gut-wrenching, eight years earlier (1884), German microbiologist Robert Koch had made an alarming discovery: cholera was waterborne.[42] Koch's revelation prodded anxious officials in other major European cities to invest in filtration systems to protect their water. Hamburg authorities, however, did nothing. Citing costs and what they considered dubious science, they ignored clear warnings and rebuffed any attempts to fight the cholera outbreak ravaging Europe. They refused to fight the death that was coming.

Those with power rejected the knowledge available to them and failed to protect the vulnerable, failed to protect their neighbors. The details may be completely different, but similar stories play out time and again. If we want to love our neighbors, we can never close our eyes when harm hovers or evil menaces. Sometimes, loving our neighbors requires actively resisting pernicious threats to our shared future.

It's no different when we seek to love our neighbors with our investments. Loving our neighbors requires recalibrating our resources to resist harm and protect the vulnerable.

THE DRAGON

As we've seen, investing is a potent but often forgotten way that our work and our life can have meaning and purpose and serve the world. Investing has real-world effects. Over the next few chapters, I want to talk about how this love-for-neighbor commitment works out concretely and to show tangible ways of how investing helps the world to rejoice. We'll discover how investing fights dragons (resists evil and oppression), tends gardens (creates goodness and flourishing), and nurtures generosity (unleashes hope and renewal).

We need to start with the dragons.

In mythical literature, a dragon often represented an ominous threat, a source of malevolent power and destruction, especially when their power was in the wrong hands. Often in ancient stories, the dragons lurked at the edges of the community's imagination, fading from concern as decades passed without any sightings out in the open. Was there such a thing as dragons? Wasn't life good and comfortable—why make a fuss? But of course, ignoring the threat just because you couldn't see it and you didn't feel the immediate danger was always a bad course of inaction. As J. R. R. Tolkien put it in *The Hobbit*, "It does not do to leave a live dragon out of your calculations, if you live near one."[43]

Dragons are real in our world. Not, so far as I know, the winged creatures breathing fire and terrorizing villagers. But there are other ravaging dragons, dragons of injustice, oppression, and greed. And it won't do us any good to leave dragons out of our calculations. The good news is that we can collectively fight the dragons, and investing can help.

We've talked about those companies that we'd be proud to own, businesses that create goodness in the world. However, there are far too many companies of another sort, corporations that use our money to exploit the poor, destroy families, pillage creation, and make humanity less human. Often, though, we're oblivious.

The last time I looked, there were roughly 162 million Americans investing in stocks, yet how many of us are aware of what we've purchased and what we're supporting?[44] If we knew all the hidden, seedy realities to many of the businesses to whom we've handed over our money, it would be difficult for us to sleep at night. Few people actively aim to harm others, yet many of us are ignorant of what corporations are *doing* with our money. Too often, those investor returns that make us smile when we open our quarterly statements arrive at the cost of someone else's sorrow and pain. This is an unjust, often hidden, oppression. And we should do everything we can to stop such cruelty. We must fight the dragons.

SINISTER SMOKE

From our beginning, we committed to resist companies that increased suffering and to support companies that fueled joy. One of our first (perhaps over-earnest) taglines was "Invest without Compromise." Given this, Big

Tobacco sat atop our not-a-chance investment list. Like anyone mildly paying attention, I knew the health risks of smoking. I'd heard the statistics on lung cancer and seen, in doctor's offices and online ads, the grotesque images of rotting flesh (numerous countries—but not the US—plaster these images right on cigarette packs). I read the statistics: Smoking kills more people than guns, drugs, alcohol, HIV, and auto accidents combined.[45] One hundred million people died from tobacco in the last century, and experts anticipate that number will increase to one billion people in the next.[46] These raw facts ought to dissuade anyone from profiting from this enterprise of death. Do any of us really want to be in the position where our retirement account grows in sync with the cancer ward?

Yet, if you dig into the largest twenty mutual funds,[47] many of them have consistently had tobacco exposure. If you look at this from the perspective of the tobacco companies, some of their largest shareholders are large American mutual funds and ETFs, including Capital Group (the portfolio manager of American Funds), BlackRock, Vanguard, and State Street.[48]

However, I discovered an evil far more sinister than a company facilitating some middle-aged man's choice to light up a Marlboro. Tobacco's real malevolence (though obscured by the industry's reformation and rebranding efforts) is how they prey on children—especially the *poorest* children in the developing world. In 2016, the World Health Organization data revealed that in Papua New Guinea 40 percent of boys and 28 percent of girls ages thirteen to fifteen use tobacco.[49] Another WHO survey from 2009 revealed that 41 percent of Indonesian boys the same age were smokers.[50] These are children whose only concern should be activities and homework, not toxic chemicals filling their lungs.

And then there was the story of Ilam Hadi, who was four when his mom gave him a few coins to buy a snack at school. Instead, he bought a cigarette. Within months, though his dad only made five to six dollars a day with odd jobs and driving a motor bike taxi, Ilam smoked two packs daily.

Over the next few years, the addiction worsened. A neighbor who ran a small shop out of her house shared how Ilam sometimes woke her at 4 a.m., pounding on her window and demanding a smoke. "Whenever he wants a cigarette," the shopkeeper told one reporter, "he looks like he is in a trance."[51] When his mom or dad wouldn't (or couldn't) give Ilam the money he demanded for cigarettes, he'd steal from his own family. "Anything he could steal in the house," his dad said, "he would sell."[52]

Years ago, I found that one of the largest mutual funds had significant exposure to a tobacco company[53] (it was the largest holding). I then saw that this fund was held by one of the largest college saving funds in America.[54]

I couldn't shake the unnerving fact of how American parents are saving for their children's future by profiting from the exploitation of the poorest children in the world. And little has changed, as over the past decade, mutual funds from Vanguard, BlackRock, and Capital Group (American Funds) have consistently been among the top investors in Phillip Morris and Altria.[55]

My friend Blake Schwarz tells the eye-opening story of the death of his grandmother, a woman he loved and admired. She was a lifetime smoker and died from cancer. As they settled her estate, Blake realized that 50 percent of her portfolio was invested in tobacco companies. She had supported, and now the family was profiting from, the very industry that killed her. This revelation sent Blake on a long journey, rethinking fundamental questions about how our investments can curb, rather than encourage, injury.

POISONED PROFIT

Considering all these complexities returns us once more to Proverbs' warning against ill-gotten gain, a serious caution against receiving any benefit from poisoned profit. It ought to be unthinkable to us to profit from someone else's suffering. Christian teaching, as well as basic virtue, moves us to work toward generosity for all, not to advance by crushing those trapped underneath us. The apostle Paul tells us we ought to "hate what is evil," certainly not to profit from it.[56] The prophet Isaiah spoke of God's fiery indignation over how many of the people had "the plunder from the poor in [their] houses."[57] There's that word *plunder* again. Maybe it's a word we should include within our financial planning lexicon. Do our investments contain plunder? Do any of our investments (as Isaiah puts it) "grind the faces of the poor?"[58]

It's not enough to merely be generous to good causes or write checks to those in need. There's a common misperception that the only moral obligation those with resources need to consider is making certain they're liberal in giving some portion of their bounty away. However, it also matters *how* we make our money. We're concerned not only with the giving we can do with our money at the end, once our wealth has been amassed—we are also concerned with the good work that we are called to do each step along the way. Remember how the Genesis story insists that our work itself has value. That value is not merely to be found through other opportunities our work (or money or investments) makes possible. The *way* that we live our life is just as important as the ideas we espouse or the causes we support. The *way* we make our money is just as important as what we do with our money once we have it.

I can't navigate these questions without thinking of my dad's oldest brother C. M. Mammen. His life casts a long shadow over my family. Though he's my uncle, because he

was twenty years older than my dad, I called him Veliyapappa (granddad). Veliyapappa was a civil engineer, and
when he was young, the whole family struggled for basic
survival. Around the time that my dad was just a boy, Veliyapappa and my dad's older siblings found my Appacha
in his bed late one evening crying because of how hungry
all his children were—and he didn't have anything to give
them. So, when a government job came open in the north
in Amlai City, Veliyapappa went. He hated being so far
from his wife and four children, but they—along with his
parents and seven siblings—needed money. As Veliyapappa
moved up the ladder, he began to understand how everything worked via bribes. Nothing moved forward without
someone sliding rupees under the table. Worse, the higher
ups expected managers to create fraudulent expenses that
they could bill to clients and skim the extra to pad their
own pockets.

When Veliyapappa asked questions, everyone shrugged.
"This is just how it works," they said. "How it's always
worked. You can't change anything. Accept it." But my uncle
couldn't do that. Core truths guided his life, and for him, his
job represented more than merely a way to make money. His
work was integral to who he was and to how he wanted to
live in the world. His work was part of how he thought he
was supposed to make the world better. He refused to profit
from dishonesty. He would not accept ill-gotten gain.

With the government job, Veliyapappa had security and the promise of a life-long pension. Eventually, he would be able to either move back home or bring his family to live with him. But instead of putting his head down and securing his future, he resigned. My uncle had no prospects and no idea how he'd put food on the table, but he did know that his work, no matter how lucrative, had to be honest. Surrendering his values for a paycheck was too high a price.

"You're foolish," his coworkers told him when he turned in his resignation. "You're a fool."

He did pay a high price. For several years, as Veliyapappa tried to start over at a paper company, his family suffered. Many nights, they went to bed with empty stomachs, uncertain if the next day would be any different. However, their home overflowed with love and joy. Veliyapappa had his integrity, and he woke each morning, knowing that he was giving his life to something honorable and that his work mattered in the right way and for the right things. My uncle believed that his work itself had to have integrity and insisted that it had to do good. And most importantly, Veliyapappa, Appacha, and Ammachi honored God. They trusted in God to be their provider.

I think often about this legacy of sacrifice from my family and how my investment decisions are so easy in comparison. However, it motivates me and fills me with a desire to live up to their integrity. Often, when I'm in a meeting poring over businesses we're considering for investment, I think about Veliyapappa. Is this a business Veliyapappa would be proud to work at? Would this business be worthy of Veliyapappa's commitment to truth and goodness?

"Money is inert, but profit is not," Jason once wrote to me. "Money is always associated with the activities by which it was derived. Profit is never value neutral; it is always ill-gotten or well-gotten (and to various degrees). Ill-gotten gain is any gain derived at the harm or expense of others. Well-gotten gain is the polar opposite: gain derived as a by-product of serving well the needs of others. The first question is not will I profit, but what is this activity—and is it in line with human good?"

Once Finny provocatively told me how he believed investors often lived like "the mafia wife." The mob boss's spouse enjoys the lavish lifestyle with posh jewelry, fur coats, and Mediterranean vacations. She knows her husband engages in unsavory dealings, but she doesn't pry too deep because she's comfortable with all the benefits. I recently watched the closing scene of *The Godfather*, a poignant visual of these hypocritical tensions. Michael Corleone (Al Pacino) had left dead bodies scattered around

New York City (including his sister's husband), and his wife Kay (Diane Keaton) knew deep in her heart that her husband was a violent man. And yet, just before the credits rolled, you see Kay standing in the living room mixing a drink as Michael and his henchmen closed the door. Kay was spared from hearing any of the nasty details of the treachery being planned a few feet from her. Kay could feign innocence. Kay could go on living her beautiful, comfortable life.

Similarly, many investors suspect that some of the companies we invest in do business in ways that contradict our values, and if we knew any of these underbelly details, it would make us squirm. So, we don't ask questions. We entrust our money to our broker or put our monthly deposit into their mutual fund on autopilot. Then we look away as our balance grows.

The metaphor haunts me. And as I've pondered the comparison, I've come to believe that some of us are also like the godfather himself. The godfather inflicts violence on one group (some rival on the other side of town), while at the same time generously supporting others (bank-rolling the community center or the new basketball court in the park of his own neighborhood). When we justify harm done through our investments because of the charity and generosity we plan to do elsewhere, we're working godfather logic. Our generosity doesn't keep us from being complicit in the injury. We take a good thing, and we turn it into evil.

God leaves no ambiguity here. He wants nothing to do with this false brand of generosity. Poisoned profit supposedly put to good use . . . God considers this hypocrisy, a farce. Deuteronomy's words are stark: "You must not bring the earnings of a female prostitute or of a male prostitute into the house of the LORD your God to pay any vow, because the LORD your God detests them both" (*both* refers to the profits, not the people).[59] As Christians, we discover that genuine love for our neighbor, which requires resisting evil and injustice, is more important than profit.

I've messaged the Proverbs passage on ill-gotten gain (Proverbs 1:10–19 ESV) as if it were written to an investor:

Original Proverb [60]	My Paraphrase for Investors
My son, if sinners entice you,	*My friend, when you invest, if sinful people entice you,*
do not consent.	*do not give in to them.*
If they say, "Come with us, let us lie in wait for blood;	*If they say, "Come along with us; let's lie in wait for innocent blood,*
let us ambush the innocent without reason;	*let's ambush some harmless soul;*
like Sheol let us swallow them alive,	*let's swallow them alive, like the grave,*
and whole, like those who go down to the pit;	*and whole, like those who go down to the pit;*

we shall find all precious goods,
* we shall fill our houses with*
*   plunder;*

throw in your lot among us;
* we will all have one purse"—*

we will get all sorts of dividends
* and profits,*
and fill our IRAs and 401(k)
* plans with plunder;*
invest with us;
we will all share the common
* purse, the common mutual*
* fund, the common ETF,*
the common hedge fund that are
* sharing in profits and divi-*
* dends and capital gains."*

my son, do not walk in the way
* with them;*
hold back your foot from their paths,
for their feet run to evil,
* and they make haste to shed*
* blood.*
For in vain is a net spread
* in the sight of any bird,*
but these men lie in wait for their
* own blood;*
* they set an ambush for their own*
* lives.*
Such are the ways of everyone who
* is greedy for unjust gain;*
* it takes away the life of its*
* possessors.*

My friend, do not go along with
* them;*
do not set foot on their paths.

These are the paths of those who go
* after ill-gotten gain.*

Proverbs, the biblical prophets, and the entirety of Scripture's collected wisdom warn us against poisoned profit, profit achieved through any means that harms the poor or traffics injustice or hinders life. We must never coddle anything that does harm. Rather, Scripture tells us to "hate what is evil."[61] Even the religious leaders who bribed Judas with thirty pieces of silver to betray Jesus refused to take back the "blood money," ruined as it was by their treachery.[62] Poisoned profit betrays any good we think we might accomplish later with our money . Poisoned profit undermines every good thing that God intends for us to do through our work and our resources.

FIGHT OR FEED?

What's most perplexing here is how often good people with good intentions get ensnared in this form of deception. Thoreau penned searing lines about the hypocrisy of givers whose largesse can, often unintentionally, shroud evil. "[I]t may be that he who bestows the largest amount of time and money on the needy," wrote Thoreau, "is doing the most by his mode of life to produce that misery which he strives in vain to relieve."[63] Even the sincerest among us, those of us with the most noble objectives, often have massive blind spots, failing to see how our everyday choices, our everyday work and investing, reveals what we *really* value.

Bill Hwang was a prominent figure in the faith and finance movement, a wunderkind who turned $200 million into a bulging $20 billion portfolio at his company Archegos Capital.[64] His faith, affirmed by those who worked closest with him, was genuine. Hwang sponsored three Bible studies a week at his offices. As a billionaire toting a backpack and driving a Hyundai SUV, he eschewed many of the trappings of wealth. And Hwang was immensely generous, launching and funding a foundation, which as of 2020 had $805 million in assets.[65] Hwang gave away millions every year to education initiatives, support for the poor, and social justice.[66] He once even went so far as to say that he tried "to invest according to the word of God and the power of the Holy Spirit."[67]

And yet these convictions failed to penetrate deeply into the most fundamental inner workings of how Hwang invested, how he did his work. Over the course of two days in 2021, Hwang lost the entire $20 billion, shuttering his company, losing billions for himself and his co-investors, and costing a painful number of jobs. The trigger for the stunning implosion was when investors and banks began to get a clearer view of how Hwang had used Archegos as (in the words of Federal prosecutors) "an instrument of market manipulation and fraud."[68] One news outlet described the debacle as "one of the most spectacular failures in modern financial history."[69]

The day the new news hit, I sat stunned as a Bloomberg alert flashed on my phone: "The billionaire behind one of Wall Street's biggest fiascos is a risk-taking, high-stakes trader, and a Christian seeking to make money in God's name." Those who've untangled the intricate layers of Archegos' investing schemes revealed a reckless level of leverage and greed, moves that were inherently at odds with the ideals of investing practiced as a form of good work and in service to the world. *Businessweek* described Hwang as "the paradoxical story of a man devoted to his church and driven to give generously, with a consuming taste for casinolike risk in his professional life."[70]

You can't, it turns out, separate your personal faith and the way you do your work. We can't separate the values we say we hold from the way we live, work, and invest. Despite good intentions (and good ideals), Hwang's investing inflicted great harm. The profit he amassed, for all the good he thought it would do, was poisoned. Instead of fighting the dragons, he fed them. In November 2024, Hwang was sentenced to eighteen years in prison for wire fraud, securities fraud, and market manipulation.

In his monumental sermon "The Use of Money," John Wesley offered deep, yet straightforward, wisdom on how we should think about profit. "Make all you can to give all you can," Wesley preached, "but make all you can without hurting yourself or your neighbor in body or in soul."[71] The *way* we make our money, the *way* we invest, is essential.

It does no good to amass vast wealth that we can then use to give away if the way we make our money inflicts injury. These businesses, the ones inflicting harm, are precisely the businesses that we need to combat. We resist destructive, unjust companies by making it painful for them to operate and grow. And yet, if we invest in them, we're doing the exact opposite. We're not fighting the dragons. We're feeding them.

AVOID OR ENGAGE?

There are many ways to fight destructive business practices and products. The most uncomplicated method is to simply refuse to invest in those companies whose products are so harmful and damaging to society. Thus, we try to drain them of the capital fueling their ability to continue. For these companies, their product itself is entirely the problem, and it's impossible to reimagine the business in any way that's healthy or constructive. The only real win is for those companies to stop making their product. These are the companies that we seek to avoid.

Tobacco fits in this category. And numerous other industries land here too—companies whose core purpose is irreconcilable with the common good. Other categories include: pornography, with its devastating harm to both employees and customers; guns, because we refuse to profit from anything that snuffs out life; abortion, due to our fundamental commitment to protect human life but also our unwillingness to profit from women's vulnerability; gambling, because of the industry's crushing impact on customers and exploitation of host communities; and companies that produce alcohol, due to the excessive profits taken from those suffering from addiction.

My colleague Ann-Marie shared her addiction story with me of waking up in a metal bed inside a cold, sterile industrial medical facility. It was Thanksgiving morning, and she had no idea how she got there. Ann-Marie learned that she had driven to the hospital inpatient clinic during a blackout. How was this even possible? She was alone, separated from her parents, husband, and children. "I was addicted to alcohol," she said. "Though it was killing me, I simply couldn't stop drinking."

Thankfully, Ann-Marie found help and became sober, but her experience compelled her to take a deep dive into the alcohol industry. Her research revealed how an enormously high percentage of alcohol sales (read: *profit*) appears to come from heavy drinkers (read: those most acutely at risk). In England, for instance, the National Institute of Health reports that 68 percent of alcohol sales revenue come from those who drink "above guideline levels."[72] The alcohol business lives off the very people who are dying from their addiction. "The alcohol industry," Ann-Marie wrote, "does not earn most of its revenues and profits from people like (most of) you, i.e., people who enjoy an occasional glass of wine. Rather, they earn most of their profits from the dysfunction, devastation, and death it brings to far too many lives. Lives like mine."

I can't conceive of any ethical way to invest in an industry whose very survival requires vulnerable, addicted people to habitually poison themselves. How can I benefit from an industry that accepts—as a normal cost of business—shattering their customers' lives and families? How can I own a business whose profit inevitably means we will suffer a staggering number of deaths (an estimated three million alcohol deaths per year), including so many innocent people, and children, killed by drunk drivers?[73]

So, there are certain companies where the product itself is what we bypass, and all we can do is refuse them at every turn. However, there are a vast array of companies who offer good products, services, and ideas—yet what they offer needs to be improved so that it can be genuinely beneficial to society. Perhaps a company has somehow gotten intertwined with an unfair business practice, or they have a blind spot about a negative impact they're having on some portion of their community. This is where we investors can do some of our most energizing, rewarding work. With these companies, we don't avoid. Just the opposite—we engage. We become advocates.

Once we noticed a financial services company that we admire list one of their credit cards with a 27.49 annual percentage rate. Worse, they offered this card with a six-months interest-free promotion, which would lead to many consumers racking up debt and then later being hit with a mountain of accumulated interest. The long-term effects on customers could be devastating. We (and other companies too) consider these terms predatory (particularly if there are no offsetting rewards or other mitigating factors), and our team reached out to explain Eventide's viewpoint. The company, caught off-guard by our report, wasn't dodgy or defensive but welcomed our research and listened to our concerns. They made no promises in the moment, but within a couple of months, they changed credit card vendors. Who can say what all their reasons were for the switch, but the fact that we were investors in their company got us in the door. And our engagement was not adversarial but worked toward mutual interests. The result was good for investors, for the company, and for the customers. That's how partnerships work.

The collective voice of investors played a significant role in the ending of the inhumanity of South African apartheid. Leon Sullivan, a Baptist pastor who served as General Motors' first Black board director, joined a group of Episcopalian investors in advocating for change with GM's plant in Port Elizabeth. The push caught fire and college students around the country began to pressure their schools' endowments and pension funds to divest all of their South African assets. Adele Simmons, president of Hampshire College and a persistent activist until apartheid's end in 1994, recalled her conversation with Nelson Mandela.

"When I met with Mandela in 1990 in New York," she explained, "he said that divestment was a crucial factor in ending apartheid. The movement against apartheid was led by South Africans, and Mandela was an inspiration throughout the decades, but the actions of U.S. investors gave the movement both visibility and legitimacy and had a decisive economic impact."[74]

South Africa's example can model how we can mobilize this same energy and assert this same moral clarity with each of our investment choices. My friend Rob Moll, a prolific writer who worked with us at Eventide for several years before dying in a tragic hiking accident, believed that investing offered one of our most potent tools for resisting evils that harm the human community. "It could do wonders for the kingdom," Rob wrote, "if individual Christians and church institutions were to restrict the billions of dollars they invest to companies that supported their values. . . . [I]t would likely do more to arrest moral decay than any amount of political involvement."[75]

Investors, using their power to fight evil and to pursue the common good, changed the lives of millions in South Africa. And there are so many stories like this. For me, one of the most profound is the story of the Uyghurs and the solar power industry. The story reveals the power of investors choosing to engage, and it inspires me to see what is possible when we combine our resources and our voice.

THE UYGHURS

As we launched Eventide, our guiding aim was to help people invest in a way that promotes human flourishing and the global common good. We wanted to use the collective power of investors to stop companies that inflict harm while helping companies that nurture good.

However, these hopes require constant diligence. The investing waters are murky, and there are a thousand ways we can unwittingly participate in the very things we hope to fight. Our investment research team constantly probes and investigates, uncovering who's benefitting from our investments and who's potentially being hurt.

In 2020, we encountered a genuinely evil story, and it raised perplexing questions for our team. We began to uncover appalling reports narrating the systemic abuse of the Uyghur people (a minority Muslim community, one of the Turkic peoples) in China's Xinjiang province. The stories were grisly: soldiers dragging away families in the night, putting children in massive state-run orphanages, sterilizing women en masse, forcing abortions, carrying at least a million Uyghurs into "vocation and re-education" camps, and conscripting thousands into forced labor. One woman who was held in custody for nine months described masked men entering their cells at night, selecting mothers and young girls to come with them to a "black room" where the men did as they pleased. "Perhaps this is the most unforgettable scar on me forever," she said. "I don't even want these words to spill from my mouth."[76]

Initially, the government detained a handful of Uyghurs suspected of ties to terrorist groups, but the aggression exploded into a systemic program that numerous countries and humanitarian organizations describe as genocide. Uyghurs are incarcerated for acts as simple as praying, owning a Koran, speaking their native language, or for having too many children. At least a million Uyghurs have been officially confined, but whole cities, with thousands of cameras and apps tracking movement, have devolved into gulags entrenched by a web of "virtual fences."[77]

As we amassed large piles of research, accounts of torture multiplied: electrocution, food deprivation, and withholding medical care. Jiang, a Chinese detective who later defected, described how officers systematically beat Uyghurs, even children as young as fourteen, during interrogation. The soldiers hung their prisoners from the ceiling, waterboarded them, and hit them with "a wrecking bar or iron chains with locks."[78] Jiang said that despite official claims, he didn't find even one of the hundreds he interrogated that he believed had anything to do with terrorism. "They are ordinary people," Jiang said.

This humanitarian horror, disturbing as it was, felt like an alternate reality far removed from us. But then information surfaced that the Uyghurs were forced to work in the mines and factories connected to the solar panel industry. China, the manufacturing hub for this industry, produces about 52 percent of the world's solar panels and up to 97 percent of the wafers required for the manufacturing process, a technology that could be critical for serving future global power needs.[79] No matter what corner of the globe you were in, wherever you saw a solar panel, the tainted supply chain meant that it was almost inevitable that those panels were in some way connected to the oppressed Uyghurs. The Uyghur crisis was no longer an alternate universe. It hit us right in our office. At Eventide, we had exposure to companies that source solar panels from manufacturers whose supply chain could have been tainted.

Looking over the piles of stories, a cavernous pit formed in my stomach. What would this mean for our investments? We had to do something, but how would we confront such a massive problem? And some members of our team worried about how our engagement might trigger a backlash from the Chinese government. While many were sounding the alarm about the Uyghurs' plight, no one was saying much about this specific problem: how the booming solar panel market was actively contributing to the oppression. A thorough, comprehensive, and profoundly vexing report (*In Broad Daylight*) put the matter bluntly: "In the Uyghur region, companies create green energy . . . but sacrifice humane labour conditions in the bargain."[80]

Over several months, we huddled together with our team, and we all knew that someone had to act. While Eventide was not invested in any companies using forced labor or facilitating the Uyghur atrocities directly, some solar energy developers were involved. Eventide had been investing in companies that own and build solar power plants, which meant that we were part-owners in companies who purchased tainted goods from a polluted supply chain. As part-owners, we could not escape our connection to the Uyghurs' misery. This would not stand. We held no illusions that our small firm could challenge such a massive evil, but we did have a dedicated team of researchers and a loyal group of investors who'd pooled their money with us. Together, we could do *something*. Together, we *had* to do something. This was a dragon we had to fight.

We didn't know what was possible, but the Uyghurs' plight was clear. Staying silent was unacceptable. I remembered Pune. I remembered Amal and Kamal. I remembered what our core principles were. If we turned a blind eye here, justifying ourselves with the greater good of clean energy and the broader impact we could make with increased profits, we would betray our core identity. We would be complicit in the oppression.

Our team was relentless, throwing themselves headlong into the logistics, the politics, and the global economics. We developed a thorough expertise in this immensely complicated international dilemma, producing an industry report that helped to reframe the debate around what's at stake. Our research began making its way into university academic reports, and Michael Posner, one of the leading business human rights professors, utilized our research in his course at NYU's Stern School of Business. Next, we crafted a market-based transition plan to leverage solar buyers' purchasing power with hopes of eventually squeezing forced labor out of the supply chain altogether. Then we took to the streets, engaging, educating, and advocating with CEOs, investors, government officials, and non-profits in dozens and dozens of conversations. We received invitations to speak at conferences and meetings around the world. The alarm was growing.

An important step for us was our direct conversations with companies who purchase solar panels. We went to the management teams to determine if they were aligned with us in pushing forced labor out of the supply chain. The CEO of one of the companies we were invested in balked, expressing ambivalence about how to weigh between stopping the destruction of the Uyghurs and slowing down the growth of clean energy. So, we divested our stake in that company.

As the atrocities came to light, companies gradually began to address their supply chain. The big win came in December 2021, when Congress passed the Uyghur Forced

Labor Prevention Act, outlawing imports connected to Uyghur forced labor. The government was closing off the spigot. Fantastic news.

However, the need for advocacy has not diminished. Rather than dismantling the operations connected to the abuse of the Uyghurs, numerous solar panel manufacturers have simply created two separate supply chains: one that serves the US and does not use forced labor, and a second one that serves other countries' markets and relies on forced labor just like it always has. This atrocity remains a live issue, and our advocacy has not wavered. As we review new companies, when we believe there may be exposure to Uyghur forced labor, we engage the companies, asking them to take direct action with their suppliers. And we have developed and supported educational resources so that investors, nonprofits, and governments can understand what's at stake, feel the weight of the Uyghurs' suffering, and work towards a solution.

But here's what's so exhilarating and hopeful: We have the capacity for this sustained, penetrating engagement because of the collective power of our investments. A major reason that many of the companies listen to investors' concerns is their fear that we will pull our money if they don't. It's just too easy for companies to turn a blind eye if doing so doesn't cost them. But together we can make it cost. This is how power works in the financial markets.

Our investments empower our capacity to speak up for the Uyghurs. Amid complex realities at home and around the globe, it's often overwhelming, and we slump our shoulders, believing there's nothing we can do. However, our investments can be a vigorous tool for good.

We've seen this over and again. Investor action has significant impact on how we build momentum to reject inhumane working conditions, impede environmental destruction, reject violent regimes, and curb those who abuse the oppressed. One *Institutional Investor* headline pulled no punches from the impact they felt was possible: "Investors Have Real Power to End Human Trafficking."[81] Our collective voice—the fact that we represent a large number of people and their dollars—enabled us to get their attention.

Investing is not merely a docile enterprise of generic numbers on a sheet that we hope will one day add up enough to allow us to provide for our family, fund our retirement, or be more generous. Investing is one of our most potent opportunities to put our faith or our values into concrete action *right now*. Investing is a way that we proclaim a fierce, unflinching no to evil, no to violence, and no to all the dehumanizing forces that we worry over but often think we have little power to resist. But we can resist evil. We can fight the dragons.

Investing Our Lives for the World's Joy

What is most important to you when you think about your investments and creating wealth? If you had to decide between faithfulness to Jesus or making a profit, which would you choose?

Tending Gardens   **6**

Investing to Help Goodness Flourish

> *A garden is a grand teacher. It teaches patience and careful*
> *watchfulness; it teaches industry and thrift; above all, it*
> *teaches entire trust. [. . .] The good gardener knows with*
> *absolute certainty that if he does his part, if he gives the*
> *labour, the love, and every aid . . . that so surely as he does*
> *this diligently and faithfully, so surely will God give the*
> *increase. Then . . . an echo of the gracious words, "Well*
> *done, good and faithful servant."*
>
> Gertrude Jekyll[82]

Previously, we've pondered Scripture's unambiguous
maxim to "hate what is evil," but that's only the starting
point. The teaching continues, insisting that we're also to
"cling to what is good."[83]

I like the word *cling*. *Cling* is a verb. It requires action.
Clinging is something we *do*. *Cling* means "to hold
together" or "to adhere as if glued firmly." So, clinging to

hope is exactly what we're up to with our vision of investing for the common good. With our investments, we embrace companies, technologies, and medicines (among many other things) that are good—good for humanity, good for creation, and good for everyone. Through our investments, we remain attached to the hope that our world can be better and that our committed resources will cultivate more peace, more justice, more beauty, more wholeness, more life, and more joy. God really wants His gardens to flourish, and our investments are one way that we can say yes to what He wants.

We want to do more than only reduce the negative effects of everything bad or degrading. We also want to be part of the world's renewal and mending. We don't want to only fight dragons. We also want to plant and tend gardens.

How do we locate companies that expand Eden, companies that bring joy into the world? Over the years, we pondered this challenge, followed the thread, and eventually arrived at an expansive, multifaceted answer, brimming with hope. We looked for those places in need of fresh ideas or solutions—or those places where good things are suffering or at risk. We then identified three guiding aims that encourage human flourishing and foster delight for all people. We are in search of companies that *develop* what's needed, *sustain* what's healthy, and *restore* what's damaged.

So, we find the companies that are:

1. working to extend, grow, or create new ways to harness resources and meet the demands of a growing and changing society (develop)
2. working to preserve, keep, or protect resources so they can continue to regenerate and provide for future generations (sustain)
3. working to make right, fix, or heal whatever is wrong or broken (restore)

This vision connects to Kerala, to Ammachi, to that question I asked from the guest house in Pune, and again praying in my parents' basement: "Why can't we do something to make the world different?"

When we realized the vast opportunity for investing to generate true value creation, a new vista opened before us: Through investing, we could participate in bringing wholeness where there was ruin, abundance where there was scarcity, and joy where there was sorrow and pain. We could use our capacity and aptitude to find good companies that have the potential to make the world better. Then we could gather resources from a community of people who share our values—and together we could help these good companies thrive.

In the previous chapter, I shared that our early tagline was "Invest without Compromise." Back then, our focus was primarily on avoiding unethical profits and standing against exploitation. Now, our tagline has evolved to

"Investing that Makes the World Rejoice." This idea is rooted in Proverbs 11:10 (NIV), which says, "When the righteous prosper, the city rejoices; when the wicked perish, there are shouts of joy," and Proverbs 29:2 (NIV), "When the righteous thrive, the people rejoice; when the wicked rule, the people groan." The wicked thrive by exploiting others, causing the poor and vulnerable to suffer under their greed. In contrast, the righteous prosper through caring for others, and their generosity brings joy to the people around them. By investing in ways that uplift others and reflect this righteous generosity, we can help create a world where everyone rejoices.

For me, investing has become one of the ways I am *doing* something. This everyday practice that's in some way connected to most of our lives (whether we have a little money or a lot, and whether we pay any attention to our investments or not) provides a powerful tool for good. Here, we have the possibility of joining others and together helping to cultivate happiness, justice, and renewal, bringing needed resources into struggling or forgotten communities so they might flourish.

Over the years, I've grown increasingly hopeful as I've seen investments help heal chronic diseases, bolster sustainable economies and good jobs, protect the weak and abused (like the Uyghurs), and push for a more sustainable future for both our own neighborhoods and for our neighbors around the globe. Investing, I've discovered, provides a way for all of us to do something, a way we can all join our efforts and help to make the world rejoice.

A VERY BIG GARDEN

Remember the first Genesis story and how, from the beginning, God has given humans a mandate to extend His beauty over the whole world? The world is God's garden, and He asks each of us (in our own ways and with our own gifts and resources) to make His garden beautiful. God has made each of us gardeners, made us responsible to tend and nurture his vast, abundant creation. God has called us to be caretakers of His world, and investing is one of the ways we are able to help His world overflow with abundant goodness.

Maybe this garden metaphor remains vivid for me because it returns me to my childhood in Kerala. In my boyhood, Kerala was Eden-like. What else was I to think with Kerala's nickname: "God's own country"? When it's been too long since I've made it back home, I ache for Kerala, for its rolling green mountains, and the sticky-hot climate. I long to inhale the clear, sweet air, walk among the lush woods, and taste the mango and pineapple, the jackfruit and papaya, passionfruit and sugar cane.

I wish I could be young and carefree again, playing outside our concrete, canary yellow bungalow. A dense forest surrounded our house: rubber trees and coconut trees, a sprinkling of cluster figs and pink bougainvillea. Even now, the fragrance of rosewood and sandalwood trees linger, rich and woody and sweet. Sony and I watched tappers move through the rubber grove, cutting slits into the bark. Thin streaks of milky gum ran like melted mascara into coconut shells. We hunted green shameplants, miniature fern-like foliage that immediately wilted and shrank after only the slightest touch. We moved like wizards, touching each plant with the tip of our finger, exercising great power over the woodlands. This was wild, enchanted country—all of it *home.* All of it ours to roam.

Even now, I still carry this ache in my heart to feel again all the warmth and love and belonging that enveloped me then. I wish I could return with my parents and siblings, walking those well-trod paths. I've tried to share this with my children, but none of this holds any meaning for them. I took them to the woods that surrounded my house, but they encountered no charm or nostalgia. The humidity, the bugs, the huge millipede, the fear of snakes—it was all too much for them. And they begged to get back inside the car. I told them that these were the same trees I touched as a very small boy and how my grandparents loved and looked after those trees. But my kids just shrugged and yawned.

If any fragments of illusion remained, my children have sufficiently shattered my Kerala idealism. Kerala was never Eden. But as a boy, I did brush against an abundance and wholeness that, I believe, reflected something of God's intentions for the world. Maybe the ways I experienced Kerala then—and the Kerala I long to experience now—reveals some small hint of God's vision for every place in the world (downtown Cleveland, the Oregon coast, the markets of Mumbai, New Zealand's volcanic plateaus).

If the world is God's garden and if all of our good and noble work becomes a way we tend to God's garden, what new possibilities open for us? How would we think differently about our work and our investments (as well as our families and our neighborhoods) if we approached them as the gardens we are tending on God's behalf? There's so much work to do. There's so much gardening to do.

IMPACT BY DESIGN

Perhaps, though, you're still wondering about a more basic question: Do our investments really make a significant impact? Can investing really alter economic trajectories or drastically affect human lives?

Yes, absolutely.

When we pondered the Eden story, we explored how our work (which includes our investing) carries its own integrity, its own intrinsic capacity for good. We don't need to perform any gymnastics to connect investing to the common good. We can simply allow our investments to do exactly what they are designed to do: to fund, expand, and promote businesses, products, or services. This is the whole reason we invest—to encourage certain businesses and hopefully share in their reward. I'm simply adding one essential distinction. I'm advocating for us to make sure that our investing expands and promotes companies that are profitable *and* good rather than ones that are *only* profitable. The axiom attributed to Henry Ford cuts through the fog: "A business that makes nothing but money is a poor business."[84]

Investments (and the companies they fund) always have impact—this fact is inescapable. The question is whether the impact will be generative or ruinous. An expansive vision for a better world far beyond our lifetime requires (among other things) investments in good enterprises and good businesses. This is not a new or novel idea. Investing has always wielded potent power. By inherent design, investments are how we move capital to create momentum, to make things happen. Investing is one of the ways we place a finger on the scales of history.

Johannes Gutenberg's Bible would never have gone to print without Johann Fust's investment. And this Bible from Gutenberg's press was a major player in Europe's radical transformation, providing "the key to unlocking the modern age."[85] *History Today* called Gutenberg's Bible "the real information revolution" and "one of the greatest advances in human culture."[86] Everyone knows Gutenberg, but there would have been no Gutenberg without Fust and his infusion of capital.

In 1492, Christopher Columbus traipsed from royal court to royal court in search of funding for his exploration. John II of Portugal, Henry VII of England, as well as King Ferdinand and Queen Isabella of Spain, all rebuffed him. Out of options, Columbus was on the verge of packing up his sails, but at the last moment, the Spanish monarchs changed their minds. The Spaniards infused capital into Columbus' venture but also had the stroke of genius to attach a profit incentive (a share in the revenue from any lands he claimed) as motivation.

It's impossible to measure how dramatically the world shifted, for good and for ill, from that one infusion of capital five hundred years ago. The door to a new future swung open. Today, the majority of Central and South Americans are Catholic and speak Spanish. Of course, the Spaniards' investment inflicted calamitous impact, too, leveling a severe warning for every investor. We still suffer the sins of colonialism. Columbus "discovered" land that was already home to indigenous peoples, enslaving many of them and infecting the continent with deadly disease. Nevertheless, there's no denying Columbus' global, history-shaping impact. All because of one investment.

For most of history, only royals and the über-elite had access to the mechanisms for investing. One hundred years after Columbus, however, a radical new democratization forever restructured the landscape, providing common citizens with the opportunity to participate. Desperate to raise capital to expand their trade routes, the Dutch East India Company concocted the audacious idea of selling ownership portions in their company to the general public. This was a tectonic shift, allowing for the possibility of reallocating power out of the hands of the ruling class and into the hands of workers and merchants. For the first time, people could collectively invest, deciding what innovative businesses they would fund. Now people could pool their money and together make economic decisions about the kind of world they wanted to help create.[87]

In the centuries since, this power shift has dynamically restructured entire industries, medical revolutions, and geopolitical politics. Grievously, the revolution has produced numerous villains. Money holds immense power to corrupt, and businesses can inflict immense harm. We *do* have to fight dragons. However, confessing that businesses can be bad for society is an easy line these days. Whenever I speak about the need to resist greedy, profit-mongering corporations, most everyone in the room nods their head. When people think of Wall Street, words like *integrity* and *common good* are rarely the first that come to mind.

However, that sad narrative tells only part of the story. I'm trying to shine light on what we might be forgetting. There's a truth that we haven't considered nearly enough: Investing can nurture good. Investing can plant good seeds, water good ideas, and watch good things grow.

One of the places where we've seen good things, astounding things, grow is in the biotech sector, funding companies developing transformative medical therapies. We have a particular passion for companies researching treatments for orphan diseases, maladies affecting fewer than two hundred thousand people. "Rare diseases are often called 'orphan' diseases," writes molecular biologist Dr. Katrin Flatscher, "because they are 'unwanted' by drug companies."[88] Flatscher explains how funding for orphan diseases is typically limited and short-term, even though researching new medicines demands both a long timeframe and large infusions of capital. Investors are sometimes skittish due to the inherent fact that there are fewer patients in need of the therapy. If profit is your solitary metric, then of course you're always going to opt for the investment that offers the fewest complications to the highest yield. However, what if profit is one (but not the only) metric? We believe it is possible to make substantial profit while also doing immense good for those who are often the most forgotten.

We've invested in a company pioneering a new class of medication to treat those who suffer from myasthenia gravis, a rare chronic autoimmune, neuromuscular disease that weakens the voluntary muscles controlling the eyes, face, mouth, throat, and limbs. You can imagine how debilitating it would be to lose your capacity to depend on such basic body movement. However, a treatment that we invested in demonstrated remarkable results, vastly improving these horrific symptoms for many patients.

In Japan, a young mother struggled with basic function and began to recede from her daily life. Unable to perform minor manual tasks, she lost her job. Isolation and despair overwhelmed her. When her children asked her to play, she could only watch. Homebound, her family went about their normal activities without her. She couldn't pick up her children; even a hug made her wince. However, within only a week or two of receiving the treatment, she regained movement she hadn't experienced for years. She got down on the floor to play with her children. She enjoyed walks, errands, and her kids' school events. When I heard of this mom's joy and gratitude, I was overcome. I would be despondent if I was shut up alone, removed from my family's everyday life. I would be euphoric if a medicine handed my life back to me.

A patient in Germany was so weak that she needed an ambulance to transport her to the doctor to receive her infusion. She required an ambulance again for her second infusion. Imagine the shock from the medical staff when, for her third treatment, she rode up and parked her bicycle near the front door.

One US patient lost sixty pounds and could barely hold himself upright. He suffered double-vision and reluctantly handed over his car keys, surrendering his independence with them. He labored to speak or swallow. His family feared the inevitable. And then his physician prescribed the same treatment. Quickly, he regained his weight. Now he carries on long, meandering conversations and eats like a horse. Remarkably, for the first time in years, he made a six-hour trip to watch his granddaughter's volleyball match. He drove while his wife sat in the front seat next to him, marveling and so happy. His daughter's words sink deep: "[This treatment] gave us our father back."

We don't invest only in research confronting orphan diseases, but also companies tackling colossal health concerns affecting millions. Schizophrenia afflicts 24 million people worldwide, leading to increased suicide rates, extreme difficulty with social functions (one estimate says that only 10 percent of US patients are gainfully employed), and a life expectancy ten to fifteen years below average.[89] Compounding the difficulty, common medications have numerous disabling side effects: massive weight gain, elevated blood pressure, the onset of diabetes, and neurological complications. The help for patients suffering from schizophrenia has progressed seemingly only inches over the past sixty to seventy years. These grim realities are why we backed one pharmaceutical company in their early stages, as they pioneered a promising therapy. This therapy is the "first drug to provide a new mechanism of action in over 70 years" and has demonstrated remarkable results with far fewer side effects.[90]

The possibilities for individuals suffering from the disease is immense, but the potential broader societal impact from this one drug is mammoth. Schizophrenia, left unchecked, overwhelms communities' mental health infrastructure and ravages families' emotional and financial well-being. If we can alleviate schizophrenia and the many forms of suffering it inflicts, we are addressing not only a chronic medical condition but also a complex web of social and individual afflictions.

For instance, estimates suggest that as many as 20 percent of the homeless suffer from schizophrenia, an astronomically higher percentage than the general population.[91] One financial advisor with connections to Eventide has taught classes at his local homeless shelter for thirty years. He's intensely concerned about the plight of the homeless community, which means he's concerned about schizophrenia. He recently shared how he had a drop-the-pencil moment when he realized that he could bring his investing and volunteer worlds together. Through investing in this company and its therapies, he could address a root problem and be part of a solution for this community in ways he'd never considered. "I'm in the shelter every week," he said, "and schizophrenia is a reason why so many of my friends are here. And now I'm realizing that I can invest in ways that help the people I've cared about for decades."

This story gets personal for me. I met Pricilla when she was seven, and I've known her family ever since. Priscilla's dad is a faithful pastor and missionary whom I've supported for years. Her dad used to regularly text me, asking me to pray for Priscilla because of her debilitating struggles with schizophrenia. One morning, she disappeared, and her family searched frantically but couldn't find her. Eventually, they did find her, slumped in the front seat of her car next to a gun she'd purchased. The disease robbed her—and all who loved her—of her beautiful, precious life. Thousands gathered for the funeral, and afterwards I sat with Priscilla's dad and mom for a couple of hours as they told me, through tears, stories about their daughter. Such heartbreak. As I heard their sorrows, I kept thinking about this pharmaceutical company we'd invested in, kept wishing the drug was already approved by the FDA. But it wasn't. Help came too late. But now I think of all the Priscillas whose stories will end differently.

Wins like this keep our fires lit. Ventures like these are how investments are supposed to work. Investments are designed for impact. Impact for good.

NURTURING THE GOOD

There are so many opportunities for our investments to tend to the world's garden and cultivate its beauty. Trucking is a notoriously tough industry, where workers often suffer from excruciating hours and shrinking wages, all the while spending months away from home.[92] To make things more problematic, the logistics required to arrange the jigsaw puzzle—the fleet of trucks and the chaos of routes, the suppliers and the weather, and the workers needed to move the cargo from one truck to another—is mind-boggling. Efficiently managing these complexities requires knowledge and expertise that can only be gained by years of experience, something that's hard to maintain when you suffer high employee turnover, as most trucking companies do. With a depleted, lackluster work force, the trickle down to customers is often delayed shipments and a high number of claims for problems with missing or damaged cargo.

These realities are so prevalent that when we identified a major trucking company doing things differently, we sat up straight and leaned forward. Deep in their DNA, this company has a resilient desire: to be a genuinely good company, tending to the diverse needs of both their customers and their employees. They pay their workers more than their competitors. They've created a well-funded training program for dock workers to move up the ladder and become drivers. They've organized their routes and hubs so that almost every one of their drivers are at home every night (a remarkable feat for a company sending shipments coast to coast). They've bought new trucks, which are better for the drivers, better for the environment (more fuel efficient and less emissions), and better for the public (older trucks are more dangerous and don't have safety features like lane departure warning systems and electronic stability control). They've upgraded warehouses and technology to streamline logistics. These forward-looking efforts have yielded high retention rates, which in turn smooths their operations. While hauling fifty thousand shipments per day across the country, they somehow still provide 99 percent of their deliveries on time, with only 0.1 percent claims due to cargo issues. Nobody matches these results. Customers are thrilled with their service, and fiercely loyal. Employees are proud to work for their company, and fiercely loyal.

This trucking company shows how doing good is also good business. Better companies, better technology, better solutions—managed properly—can meaningfully contribute to the common good.

Often, I think of my childhood in Kerala and how simple advancements that are unremarkable now would have saved so many lives. Neighbors and family members suffered from frightening diseases and debilitating health concerns that we now treat by snagging a pill from the

Walgreens drive-through. I had a friend, Julie, who lived up the dirt road from our house. She had a swing set in her yard, which made her house a wonder to Sony and me. I remember one traumatic weekend when Julie's family went to a carnival. Julie got her hands on a cheap toy, a plastic pipe with a balloon attached to the end. The idea was to blow on the pipe and watch the balloon swell. However, Julie sucked in, swallowing the balloon whole. The rubber lodged in her throat as she panicked. Julie clawed for every little bit of oxygen. In such a crisis today, we'd grab our cellphones. Within minutes, an ambulance, lights flashing and siren wailing, would arrive. This hospital on wheels would carry every imaginable medical contraption. And Julie would be alive.

We enjoy a vast array of technological advancements that were unimaginable only a couple of decades ago. Commonplace remedies that barely evoke a yawn with us would have been revolutionary marvels in Kerala. When we moved to the US, I didn't comprehend that I would lose contact with my grandparents. But we had no Internet, and international phone calls were exorbitantly expensive. I went years without seeing my grandparents' faces, and I rarely even heard their voices. How different would my experience have been—how much more connected would I have stayed to my home and history during those years—if we'd had Zoom or Facetime? Now, with a few swipes, the face of a person thousands of miles away appears right in front of us.

The automotive industry is pursuing all kinds of groundbreaking innovations. I've kept a steady eye on the growth of autonomous driving. While engineers certainly need to continue improvements that will make this technology safe for broad, everyday use, the potential for saving lives is massive. Every year, from Tokyo to Portland, 1.35 million people lose their lives on our roads. In the US, traffic fatalities are the number one killer for people aged one to fifty-four, more than cancer, heart disease, or homicide.[93] Human error causes most of these deaths, and we can stop a lot of them.

I'm sure that on some subconscious level, I'm drawn to this technology because I've experienced up close how one bizarre, completely preventable human error can shatter a family. Years ago, I volunteered as a youth director at a church in Dallas, and one evening I answered the phone and sat stunned as I heard the crushing news. An elderly woman got confused and turned her car down the wrong side of the road, striking the sedan that carried the entire family of one of our students. The disoriented woman careened into this family's vehicle, leaving a crushed mangle of metal and bodies. The mom and their oldest son died at the scene. Their youngest daughter, only five, was paralyzed. There are few words to say when grief and horror strike. If either of those vehicles had been fitted with one of the emerging safety features, a family could have avoided tragedy.

Not every advancement or new technology is good—not by a long shot. This reality stokes even more the call for increased engagement, certainly not less. We need to actively implement diligent, wide-eyed wisdom and hawkish discernment. We need values that will guide us into the future. And then we need collective investments that put our values to work. This is how we use our investments to "cling to what is good."

PULLING WEEDS

Sometimes all we need to do to tend the garden is plant good seeds and then water. It's the same with our investments: Sometimes we simply need to identify good companies and then come alongside them with resources to help them thrive. Other situations, however, require more. Sometimes we need to encourage a good company to be an even *better* company by advocating for them to more fully integrate the values they insist they have. Every gardener will tell you that healthy gardens usually require pulling weeds every now and then.

Investing is a partnership. We are, after all, owners whose whole purpose is to provide support. As investors, we can keep an eye out for where companies are inconsistent with their stated mission or lose sight of core principles amid a swiftly changing landscape. In conversations, we can explain to a company our values in a holistic frame, demonstrating how the ethics we support applies to questions and issues that they might not recognize at first glance. All investors have the power to engage companies by writing letters to senior management or the investor relations department. Investors also hold the power to vote on major decisions such as electing board members, and investors can even show up in person at the annual shareholder meetings to express feedback.

Investors that are investing in mutual funds and ETFs should encourage the portfolio management teams to engage with the companies in the portfolio. I like the weeds analogy because weeds are nuisances that only get in the way, robbing resources and draining energy from the abundant harvest we hope to enjoy. When crabgrass or pigweed takes root, then somebody needs to get the hoe and clear it out. Similarly, investors with a clear-sighted vision of a company's purpose and what the company offers the world, advocate to clear out whatever impedes those hopes.

This work requires diligence and persistence. Just like in gardening, if we are idle and unengaged with our investments, weeds will take root and eventually overwhelm the entire plot. We must be constant and attentive to our weeding so that companies grow and prosper into the beautiful, vibrant organizations they are meant to be. Investors, like gardeners, do the small, necessary work so that everyone can enjoy the fruit when it's time.

Once, we had a stake in a real estate investment trust, and discovered they'd provided a grant and offered matching employee contributions to a nonprofit that provides elective abortions. We shared our concerns with the company and discovered that the "grant" was the loan of an overseas facility to help the nonprofit's COVID relief efforts, providing space to store personal protective equipment and bedding. We were proud of them for stepping up during a medical emergency but were troubled by the nonprofit's other initiatives. The real estate trust explained that no employee had ever used their matching program for this group and reiterated that their philanthropy centered on education and the environment, so they'd happily close this troubling option. The conversation was collaborative not combative. We engaged the company with our concerns, and as a result, this business we admire adjusted. A good company became an even better company.

We have conversations regularly with all kinds of companies, where we explain our hopes for partnering with them to pursue the common good. And since we speak for thousands of investors, our voice carries far more weight than if just you or I were trying to have that conversation. Our presence allows us to speak up when proposals or products contradict our ideals. Also, our backing bolsters companies who want to do the right thing but need support when opposing forces conspire to get them to cut corners or relinquish their ideals.

Businesses are more than mere profit machines. "Business plays a key role in providing creative and accessible solutions for some of our most pressing needs," writes Associate Portfolio Manager Faina Rozental-Behrer.[94] As investors, we collectively provide the resources required for good businesses to exist, and through this partnership, we play a part in tackling some of those pressing needs.

We're creators, tending this marvelous garden of a world. God invites us to do our part so that the world might bloom and flourish. God gives us our place and our many forms of work and tells us that what we do genuinely matters. Author Winn Collier names our God-given vocation: "May we, with whatever gifts and resources God has given us, be tender, creative, and wise gardeners in our acres of creation."[95] We are responsible to use whatever skills and opportunities we have, responsible for the place we call home, responsible for the neighbors who share this home with us. We have an opportunity to make the garden beautiful.

Investing Our Lives for the World's Joy

Consider the companies you own in your portfolio. How are these companies impacting not only your own returns or the companies' stakeholders but also helping to make the world more just, good, and whole? Are these businesses bringing the world joy or sorrow? Reflect on how these businesses impact the world economically and morally.

Unleashing Generosity 7

A Life of Open Hands

> *"Well, the God I believe in isn't short of cash, mister."*
>
> U2, "Bullet the Blue Sky"

I keep returning to the garden imagery, the idea that our life and work, and certainly our investing, can help to create a flourishing life for others. Gardens evoke a lot of meaning for me because in Kerala gardens weren't merely ornamental or a hobby but an integral part of how we sustained our families and cared for the community. Many of us grew food for a straightforward purpose—we needed to eat. But everyone had this same need, and gardens were a resource for how neighbors generously shared food from their little plots of soil. The bounty from the gardens was a way we watched out for each other. Okra and long string beans, tomatoes and cabbage, tapioca and spinach, ivy gourd and bitter gourd. There was abundance, plenty—and the gardeners' generosity created and sustained an entire, interwoven communal structure. We used the resources entrusted to us in our gardens for the good of everyone.

This is another reason why I think the garden metaphor works so well for considering how God has created us to use our skills and energy to do good work in the world—and yes, for how our investing *works* in the world too. When we invest, we take the resources entrusted to us—those resources we work for and tend to over many years—and deploy them for the good of everyone. We invest to take care of our own future and family, of course, but it doesn't stop there. Our investing is part of the work we do, this grand mosaic of a life we live, and our work and our life have profound purpose and meaning. We have the joy of being responsible not merely to provide for ourselves but to participate in God's intention to make a thriving world. Generosity is interwoven into everything we're talking about in these pages. Investing, understood rightly, is generous because it unleashes hope and renewal for a wide circle, for people we won't ever know. We don't work or live (or invest) only for our good, but for the common good. Investing is one way that we, like Kerala gardeners, live generously.

A GENEROUS STORY

I've tried to set our conversation around investing within the broader context of a much larger story—the story of how God intends for our lives to make significant contributions to the world. Many of us are ambivalent or dissatisfied with our work because we think that our jobs are mundane, purposeless. We don't recognize how our everyday labor contributes to the world's joy and renewal, to the common good—and this vacuous existence, the monotonous hamster wheel of earning a paycheck to accumulate more stuff we don't really need or even want, disillusions us. We are intended to experience and contribute so much more than this. Deep in our souls, we know we were made for generosity and creativity, not selfishness and insular tedium. It's a gloomy existence if we think that our lives consist of little more than grabbing what's ours (often at another's expense), having a few years of retirement, and then getting laid in a coffin and buried under six feet of dirt.

A tight, self-obsessed focus, rather than giving us more joy and delight, only robs us of the meaningful life God intends for us. "Anything you do not give freely and abundantly," writes Annie Dillard, "becomes lost to you. You open your safe and find ashes."[96]

When I worked for Mellon, I could see how I was prospering, but Amal and Kamal were suffering. In another job that I held for a little while, all I saw stretching in front of me was decades of grinding to bill clients as many hours as possible, so I could climb the corporate ladder and maybe one day become a partner where I'd reach the pinnacle: an office with a better view and better stock options. Even in high school when I was selling Cutco knives, I couldn't bring myself to ask any of my family or friends to buy a knife set that cost over $1,000. They couldn't afford it, and I felt like those exchanges would have been using people, not offering them something that was good for them, all to make a profit for myself and my employer. This was probably the first time I felt that tension (though I didn't have the language yet) of extracting value *from* others rather than creating value *for* others. After selling two or three of the cheapest knives and scissors, I quit that job.

Most of us yearn for our work to be more than making a living, certainly more than greed or self-interest. We long to engage in work that contributes to human flourishing. We long for our lives to be generative, abundant. And there are so many ways to be generous. When an investor invests in a cancer drug that will likely yield a lower profit return— but she does so gladly because she believes the world needs this therapy—that's generosity. When a graduate takes a job as an elementary school teacher, having a concern for children's future rather than a high-paying Wall Street job, that's generosity. We want our entire lives to be generous.

It's important to say here that not everybody has the same ability to think as comprehensively about their impact on the world through their work. When you are simply trying to survive and feed your kids, then that responsibility rightly consumes your energy. When my family landed in the US, my parents had no time or bandwidth to think about much more than grabbing the first jobs they could get. Their impact on those in need began with their immediate circle, providing elemental necessities for my siblings and me. However, they served other neighbors as well. My mom responded to an opening for a nursing home aid, work she stuck with for twenty-five years. Every time my mother bathed one of the elders in her care, her hands poured tangible love over that feeble body. My dad bagged groceries at Purity Supreme, picked up odd jobs painting, and eventually became a mental health aid. When my dad added beauty to someone's home or sat beside an agitated patient to calm them, his work was noble, valuable. My parents' work offered value to the world, and it's work God holds in high regard (even if our culture doesn't). However, my parents also took these jobs because they had to—the family needed food and a roof over our heads.

Today, I am in a place with more agency and far more choices in the decisions I make about my work; whenever we find this freedom, we should use it for good. Similarly, most of us who invest in the stock market have a lot of choices about where we invest. We have a much broader capacity for contemplating the kind of impact we hope to make. To whom much is given, much is required.

Earlier, I shared my hope that we'll reconsider the short-sighted assumption that investing for the common good primarily focuses only on making money for the purpose of then giving a significant portion of that money away. How we make our profits is just as much a part of our generosity as what we do with the profits after we've pocketed them. We must consider how the actual *ways* we make our money can either encourage good or embrace evil, and how the ways we make our money either hurts or helps our neighbors. The "work to give" approach misunderstands God's purpose of work—and provides an insufficient (and, I'd argue, *unfulfilling*) aim for our life.

In multiple places, Scripture instructs those of us who own the business (and remember: Investing is a modern way that many of us own small pieces of a business) to watch out for the workers' and the whole community's well-being through the actual work of the business itself. Deuteronomy, for instance, instructs owners to pay workers their wages before sunset because the regular flow of pay creates the infrastructure for the laborers' well-being (and thus the infrastructure and well-being of the whole community). Similarly, Malachi rebukes those who trim and scheme and refuse to provide a good, sturdy wage to workers, an act of sabotage to the web of communal life that the prophet envisions.[97] Good work, good business, good investing—each of these are themselves acts of generosity.

GENEROUS JOY

With all this, though, I never want to minimize the necessity of living with open hands and concretely giving money away. Providing financial resources to care for a wounded, destitute traveler was how the Samaritan loved his neighbor. And our open-handed generosity is one way we love our neighbors too.

We need spontaneous giving in response to acute crises (a hurricane or a child's leukemia treatment), but we also need intentional, sustained generosity that addresses systemic maladies and injustices while helping to underwrite a new future. Generosity ignites mammoth potential to bless the world. And for those seeking to follow the way of Jesus, generosity is essential, a non-negotiable theme that orders our lives. We make money, and, yes, we are then supposed to give money away. And when we invest wisely, our capacity for generosity grows.

I find giving to be such a profound source of joy. The generosity I encountered through my family as a child (from helping a hungry family to donating land for a cemetery) was nothing exceptional, just our normal, everyday practice. It was natural to help, to say yes with warm and eager hearts. Generosity was a delight, not a duty. This posture shaped me. Even when I was living in my parents' basement and searching for a job, I found ways to support a Nigerian widow and her three children who were part of our house church. On Tuesdays, I visited the Boston Commons with a friend to pass out food to the homeless and talk to people about our faith. It pained me to see people in need of something so simple as a sandwich and a place to sleep. On Fridays, we'd serve food at a housing community in East Boston. I'm not describing some grand spiritual practice but rather what I'd discovered to be a joyful way to live.

Giving provides authentic pleasure, but I also understand giving as my responsibility. How can I pass by a suffering person when I can help? As a Christian, I know that my resources aren't really mine. Whatever I have is God's, and I'm just responsible to manage it well. It's easier to hold a loose grip on something if you know it's not really yours to begin with.

For my wife Jaunita and me, one of our deepest joys has been the opportunity to join others in pouring energy, heart, and funds into founding the Darsha Academy, a residential girls' high school in Bengaluru (Bangalore), India. Limited access to quality education inflicts and then entrenches social inequality throughout India, perpetuating the cycle of poverty, discrimination, and disparity. Darsha opens elite educational opportunities for those who would otherwise be locked out. Recently, several Darsha families invited me into their homes. In every conversation, my eyes went moist. These young women are bright and courageous, brimming with ideas. However, due to their caste or socioeconomic status, the doors would have stayed slammed shut. These girls would have never had the chance to demonstrate their intelligence and skill and never been encouraged to prepare to take their place as leaders, contributing to their full potential.

On one visit, we sat on blue plastic chairs under a sheet of rusty tin hanging from the back of a two-room shanty. An oscillating fan fought valiantly against the heat and the flies. The family served us plates piled high with the most amazing spiced fried chicken. We listened as the dad described what was now possible for his daughters, prospects that a few years ago seemed a fairy tale. Similar stories played out in house after house. These young women imagine a radical new future, which, in turn, means the future of each of these families (and all the generations to follow) will also fundamentally transform. This ripple effect astounds me.

How could my work ever be more fulfilling than seeing the marvel of this personal, multi-generational impact? Some days I think that helping to start Darsha, even more than helping to start Eventide, might be my most personally fulfilling work. I find myself estimating my income for the coming year because I'm calculating how much we can give. I'll have in mind how much money Darsha needs for the next phase of our plan to build the very best school for these women and their families, and since Jaunita and I are the source of funding, I feel both the desire and the responsibility to get us there. I imagine these girls' faces as I work through their names, remembering their hopes and their futures. And then, energized by all that's possible, I get back to work. Being a part of creating Eventide, with its breadth and scope, will of course have a far greater impact than a single school in Bangalore. Still, the joy of participating in Darsha, serving girls and their families connected to my childhood home, floods me with gratitude.

I encounter people everywhere who find this unfathomable joy in giving. It's like a club of disparate individuals who've all found this countercultural recipe for happiness. One person only has a few dollars a month to help support an orphan or donate to their church's food bank. Another person writes large checks to anchor colossal projects. It's never about the amount but the heart. In Scripture, Jesus marveled at the widow who gave two mites (something like a penny) because she gave what she could. She had a generous heart. I heard one teacher say that Jesus was so impressed with the widow, not because of how much she gave but because of how little she kept for herself. Everyone can cultivate a generous heart. Everyone can join the widow and her mites.

GENEROUS BUSINESS

Our hope is that as we become generous people, we in turn will create generous businesses and institutions. This is how societal transformation happens. At Eventide, we donate a large part of our company profits to charities. We also have what we call the Empowerment Initiative where we directly allocate a portion of our assets under management to socially impactful investments, targeting the most vulnerable populations in the US and internationally.[98] These investments support small businesses (many founded by women in Africa and South America), tackling issues of renewable energy, affordable housing, community development, microfinance, and environmental sustainability. Imagine the global sea of change if something comparable became a regular corporate practice.

One of the ways this initiative has blessed me is to hear the stories of lives transformed through this investment. In 2023, we were able to commit capital to HOPE International, an organization with a long, successful track record that works in some of the most underserved areas.

Eventide has also provided funding for World Vision through their VisionFund, a microfinance effort focused on lifting families out of poverty and expanding financial inclusion in local contexts around the globe. I'm proud of our involvement with HOPE International and the VisionFund.[99]

We've invested in a family farm in Dodowa on the outskirts of Accra, Ghana. Elkana and his wife Paulina launched a business raising chickens but could only afford a few birds. "I started this [poultry] business on a small scale," Elkana explained. "My dream was to expand and grow the business, but it was a struggle due to financial constraints." We helped to provide a series of loans, and over time, they've reinvested their profits, adding more chickens as well as a variety of crops to build a sustainable enterprise. They've repaid each loan along the way.

The impact of Elkana and Paulina's farm on the entire community is where you start seeing the domino effect of how a good business helps everyone flourish. They've added four permanent and three seasonal workers. They've also converted the footpath to their village into a road for vehicles, opening better links to the city for the entire village. Elkana and Paulina have a steadfast commitment to share the success of their thriving business with their community. "We have a duty to help," Elkana said. "So, we are trying our best to help people in the community by providing food crops from the farm to the needy. People come to me for all kinds of support, which my wife and I are able to provide. We recently paid a hospital bill for one of my casual workers and also paid two-years' rent for a widow. I also support people with school fees and other kinds of help that I can offer." Elkana and Paulina are not merely recipients of generosity but fueling generosity themselves. Generosity transforms, recreates, and catalyzes a new future for a wide, wide circle.

Another story comes from Myanmar. Phyu Phyu is married and the mother of three children, and since 1996, she has served as a licensed nurse and midwife in the Hmawbi Township clinic. For twenty-seven years, Phyu has labored under the strain of an overwhelmed health-care system. Where she lives, there is only one nurse per ten thousand people, and the maternity ward doesn't have enough space to serve all the mothers who come to see her.

For years, when the township clinic was packed or when women needed help in the middle of the night, patients would find her and knock on her door. Phyu even delivered babies in her home. Eventually, Phyu Phyu got a license and opened her own clinic, working in the evenings after her shifts at the township clinic were done. Can you imagine her exhaustion?

Soon, her new clinic was bursting at the seams, but the next hurdle was the woeful lack of medical supplies. "There are around five hundred households in each village," Phyu said. "But there aren't enough pharmacy shops stocked with needed items, especially around my village." Seeing the need, what else would this relentless entrepreneur do but use her own savings, monthly salary, and profit from the clinic to open a pharmacy, expand her maternity clinic, and hire more assistant nurses to serve the patients? Phyu's a powerhouse.

But the funding she could manage on her own wasn't enough, and the loan which our investors supported gave her the funds she needed for her expanding practice. She's now serving even more clients, and with the increased revenue, she's hired three nurses and two other staff. This means that more people's medical needs are cared for, all while creating good jobs and steady livelihoods for a growing number of families.

Phyu Phyu is gratified by the work that she does and believes she is making a real difference in her community. She hopes one day she can even pass her vision on to her children. "My youngest daughter wants to be a doctor," said Phyu Phyu proudly. "It makes me feel like she will be the one who will follow the path that I have walked."

Do you see how generosity really can create entire new possibilities for individuals, for families, for villages and cities and nations? Remember, generosity is not a grand gesture or an isolated act but our posture, a way of life. We have seen firsthand the impact our generosity can have, but we certainly do not have it all figured out. I hope you are encouraged by these stories and see the real ways our capital changes lives.

In fact, the stories that move me most are the stories of common individual people who are both generous and unassuming. Since true generosity is a matter of the heart, we don't give so that we can polish our spiritual reputation or get our name plastered on a university's new science building. Truly generous people aren't trying to impress others. Eugenia Dodson died two weeks shy of her 101st birthday. Widowed in 1949, Eugenia worked for years as a beautician and lived frugally, alone in her small condo. At Eugenia's death, her neighbors and friends were shocked when they learned she had amassed $35.6 million. And they were even more shocked to learn she left her entire fortune to fund cancer research and diabetes. "She was dead-set on doing good for humankind," a friend explained. "She had a big heart."[100]

Many of us have big hearts, but only a few of us have $35 million to give away. However, each of us can be generous with whatever we have. Our little bits of generosity, collected within the economy of grace, are a concrete way that we actively pursue God's hopes for the world. Generosity, living openhandedly with our money, is one joy-infused way that our investments can love our neighbors, seeding hope and spreading renewal far and wide.

Investing Our Lives for the World's Joy

How are you practicing generosity through your work, giving, and investing? Are you giving a minimum or sacrificially? Do you ever accept lower compensation or less immediate benefit to do work that blesses others (teaching, non-profit, etc.) or support those who do so? Do you ever accept less financial return so that you can invest in a business that blesses others?

Embracing Joy　　　　8

The Power of We

> *A great many a drop of water will create*
> *a creek.*
>
> Giovanni Morassutti[101]

At the beginning, I said this would be a book about joy. I hope you've experienced my delight along the way and the abundant gratitude I feel for learning how to align my work with God's vision for the world. I've encountered enough pain and sorrow to feel the ache for how the world ought to be. Thankfully, I've also experienced the fulfillment and pleasure that comes from joining God's intentions to make the world right. Our lives are not meaningless blips on the vast canvas of history. The lives we live, the unique passions we carry, the work we do—all of this can contribute to the world's flourishing. Isn't that something? This is a recipe for joy.

In my work, it's been liberating to discover how investments can make a direct, significant impact toward making the world more just, more beautiful, and more of the world we all long to experience. I hope that you, with your own unique gifts and skills and relationships, have caught some renewed vision for how your own work—whatever it might be—can also have a meaningful impact. We need you. Your work matters. We experience real joy as we embrace this truth.

This returns us to the large thread of joy woven through these pages—the call to participate in helping the whole world experience gladness and goodness. Our efforts, our work and lives, and our investments are each contributing to God's purposes for every person, for the whole of creation. God wants the world to be filled with joy, and God has invited us to help Him in His project.

Hopefully, this divine invitation feels inspiring and exhilarating, but maybe it feels overwhelming too. Thankfully, we're not aiming for heroic efforts but everyday faithfulness. Rebekah Ashworth, who works in communications at Eventide, expressed the heart of this:

> The draw to "investing that makes the world rejoice" for someone like me is that I don't have to be brilliant, talented, or adventurous to contribute beyond my immediate sphere of influence. I can be faithful day-to-day, in the work God has given me and the places He has put

me, and I can know that faithfulness in those "menial" things, like where we put away a little extra money, actually has both a temporal and an eternal impact. I don't know if that will resonate with everyone, but it is encouraging to me!

Joy. *Our* joy. The *world's* joy. It's all intertwined.

Yet some of us may still worry that our small investments are like a single drop in the great sea of the global economy. The needs are too overwhelming, the troubles are too vast, and the concerns too intractable. The truth is that our efforts are futile . . . *if* we're doing this on our own.

But we're not meant to do this on our own. We're not meant to heave all the world's weight on our frail shoulders. Thankfully, God carries the world's weight, and then God invites us to join Him as He enacts healing, justice, and hope. "It is not my job to save the world," wrote Tyler Wigg-Stevenson, "but I can serve the mission of the God who has already done so."[102]

And here's the extraordinary vision that's captured me: Our investments are one of the ways we can combine our resources and collectively join God in spreading healing and hope. Our investments are one of the ways we can link together and love our neighbors with wide open arms. The money we collectively put to work through business can slowly, methodically serve neighbors two streets over as well as those in a village on the other side of the globe. It's remarkable how investing allows us to pool our resources and love all kinds of neighbors in all kinds of places, especially those who are most vulnerable.

But we can only do this through collective action. We're only able to move into these spaces and have these conversations because we speak for a wide swath of individual investors. Our hope is to partner with others to fundamentally change the playing field, a vision none of us could ever reach on our own. But together, we *can* tackle mammoth problems. Pooling our investments together and then using our collective advocacy, we can love our neighbors, particularly those most vulnerable. When any of us think of only our own resources, energy, and skill—all in isolation—it can feel hopeless or exhausting. Together, though—that's different. There's genuine power in *we*.

THE WEDDING

Whenever I think about the wonder of people banding together to address the needs of their neighbors, I always return to one story from my childhood. In our traditional culture, marriages were arranged, and my dad's oldest sister was to marry a young man from a nearby village. However, his family required a dowry of 1,500 rupees, an unthinkable sum when the price of a cow was 50 rupees. So, my family concocted a plan. They would also arrange a marriage for my dad's oldest brother, and my grandparents would request 1,500 rupees from the future daughter-in-law's family. The brother's engagement ceremony would be at 10:00 in the morning. Then we'd turn around and give the rupees to the sister's in-laws in a ceremony at 3:00 in the afternoon. It would be tight, but the puzzle could fit.

However, 10:00 came and went, and the bride's family never showed. 11:00, noon, 1:00. Nervous guests glanced out the window. Appacha paced, wiped his brow, worried his hands, and stepped outside to peer down the road, trying to catch any sign of hope. Gossip of the catastrophe spread like brushfire. The 3:00 family gathered nearby, but hearing the bad news, they prepared to return home to their village.

"Come, come," my grandfather pleaded. "We'll figure it out. We will get the money. Come, have something to eat or drink while we make plans for what to do." But there was only shame and confusion. Everything was unravelling.

And then, one friend knocked at the door, followed by two more. Soon, a stream of neighbors lined up, stretching into the yard. Most came with a few rupees. Some came with one hundred. One man brought 500 rupees. The shock could not have been any greater if he'd delivered all the gold from Fort Knox. No one in my family could imagine anyone so wealthy that they'd have 500 rupees . . . in cash . . . just lying around their house.

The experience was like the closing scene from *It's a Wonderful Life* when Bert and Harry and Annie and the whole town of Bedford Falls showed up in the Bailey living room on a snowy Christmas Eve to pool their dollars and save George Bailey. Only our story wasn't a Hollywood script. Over one hundred families, even the poorest, contributed what they could until there was a pile of 1,500 rupees. Our neighbors refused to let my family weather the crisis alone.

That evening, the 10:00 family finally showed up, shamefaced and apologetic. They'd had their own financial deal go sour, scuttling their dowry too. Appacha told them not to worry, that they were all in the same boat. Over the next few weeks, my uncle's in-laws paid their portion, which Appacha then used to pay back all the friends who'd saved the day.

I've never experienced the force of neighborly love so powerful as this. And even now as I'm writing, I'm struck by the fact that I've spent a chunk of my life starting an asset management firm, which is essentially a bunch of people (some who have a lot to invest and some who have a little) pooling their money together to address a financial need. An investment fund does not exist merely for altruism and goodwill (like the neighbors combining their rupees to save two weddings), but why shouldn't we follow more of this impulse—using our combined resources to enact good while also making a healthy profit? Shouldn't everything we do, even our investing and our profit, promote the common good? Shouldn't everything we do practice the love of our neighbors?

If we coalesce our lives and our work around a love for our neighbors, can you imagine the world that might be? What if we rolled up our collective sleeves, each doing our small bit? What if we combined our collective energy, commitment, and resources toward our common purpose for this good and just future?

What if we participated in helping this aching world rejoice?

Take the Next Step

We're giving our lives and work to investing that makes the world rejoice. We would love for you to join us. To get started, visit goodinvestor.com.

APPENDIX

But What About . . . ?: Pondering
Common Questions

One thing I love about my job is the conversations I have with people who genuinely desire to do good things in the world. Often, when I'm sharing the investment philosophy that I've offered in these pages, similar questions arise— lots of really good questions. I wanted to list a few of the most common ones and tell you how I think about them. Actually, these responses are not just from me but represent a collaborative effort, a combination of my own musings as well as thoughts from Jason Myhre, Finny Kuruvilla, and other friends and colleagues who have helped to shape my thinking.

Obviously, these answers aren't final. Real life often presents complex dilemmas and requires patient discernment. I hope that what you find here (in this whole book really) will encourage you to ponder these things for yourself and arrive at your own convictions.

If I invest based on my values, won't my investments underperform?

Over short periods of time, you'll see variance up or down, but generally, over long periods, the returns are roughly the same. A recent comparison of an S&P 500 Index portfolio screening out companies widely considered objectionable by values investors performed slightly better than the index itself.[103]

Jon Hale, head of Sustainability Research at Morningstar, summed this up well:

> The idea that sustainable investing is a recipe for underperforming is a myth. Like most myths, there is a kernel of truth to it—that exclusionary screening for nonfinancial reasons can limit portfolio performance. We found evidence in the research that exclusionary screening can have a negative effect. But the research also finds intriguing evidence of a positive [values-based] inclusion effect, which is bolstered by company-focused research suggesting that firm-level sustainability performance is associated with better financial outcomes.[104]

Basically, Hale is saying that whatever we give up by excluding certain kinds of business, we gain on the other end by using these same criteria to identify the dynamics that point to healthy, successful businesses. If we screen out a tobacco company, for instance, sure—we'll not make any of that tobacco profit. However, we'll also (on top of staying true to our value of doing good rather than harm) have a new lens by which to find those companies poised for sustainable growth.

Fred Reichheld explains research[105] where he showed that the single most powerful leading indicator for a company's future financial success is not its balance sheet or earnings or its price/earnings-to-growth ratio. Rather, the essential determinant is the degree to which a company serves its customers. In fact, he proposes a very specific metric to predict how well a company will do. That metric is the degree to which a company seeks to serve its customers rather than maximize its profit. Being a good company is not a hindrance but instead leads to health and sustainable profits.

Investing has a design and purpose: to fuel business. And business itself has a purpose: to create good products that serve others and to create those good products using good practices. Business is a social enterprise affecting all the business's neighbors: customers, employees, vendors, the communities where they operate, the natural resources they use, and the wider society with whom they are relationally entwined. Everything a business does needs to be enacted with justice and stewardship toward everyone they serve. When investors analyze whether a business they support and profit from is underperforming, the business needs to be judged against the full scope of that business's purpose.

This wider understanding of a business's purpose helps rather than hinders wise evaluation. Good businesses that are doing what they were intended to do, including making healthy profit, make the best long-term investment. Conversely, if we only look at immediate financial returns, that myopic focus might mask deeper, systemic problems hidden out of sight. Too often, we fail to factor in the cost or risk incurred when we evaluate a company's performance only by their profit ledger.

We know there's more than one way to make a profit. We can profit by pursuing justice and stewardship, or we can profit through exploitation and greedy shortcuts. If we are only looking for immediate monetary profit with no consideration for any other factors, we won't know the underlying engine for how those profits are achieved. However, if we investigate what's behind the profits and think comprehensively about the nature of business and how business creates value (and how it can operate sustainably over long periods of time), then we discover a much deeper, more just and viable, means to find and evaluate those companies that will be truly profitable in the long run.

Even if these realities weren't true and there was an inevitable cost to bear without any offsetting upside, I think we should still be willing to make sacrifices for those things that we believe are right and consistent with our morals. Is it worth a percentage point in return to follow our convictions and our sense of what's good for our neighbors and the world? Is something genuinely of value to us if we aren't willing to sacrifice anything for that supposed value?

We may be tempted to narrow our focus too much on the tiny picture when we're up to something far larger, a cause far more substantial for our own integrity and for the common good. We can concentrate on financial benchmarks and completely miss the joy of participating in human flourishing by allocating capital in ways that bring about good. We could be a loan shark, or we could give a loan at a discount to the same person struggling in poverty as a way of making a profit while also helping a family. What type of people do we want to be?

But I'm only a small investor. If I have a small amount invested into a mutual fund or a massive multinational corporation, how can my little bit possibly matter?

When we look at our dollars tossed into the vast expanse that is the global market, it can feel insignificant. Especially when you think about mutual funds and ETFs, where we own miniscule pieces of maybe one hundred companies, it's common to look at our small part, which seems so diluted, and to think that it's entirely inconsequential. How can our tiny thimble of water dropped into the massive ocean make any difference at all?

I believe the reality is just the opposite. The power of mutual funds and ETFs is that it makes it possible for small, everyday investors to pool resources and have collective influence that we could never have alone. Someone might have a couple thousand dollars in an Eventide fund, and it may by itself seem paltry. However, pooling resources alongside thousands of investors offers a platform to advocate for positive change to a company's management team.

Any social action, from political change to raising the money to build an orphanage in a struggling country, requires lots of people to collectively act, each one doing their small part. It would lead to nihilism if we applied this logic of individual actions making no difference to everything else that we do. If we look at individual contributions in isolation, it feels impossible. However, the massive scale creates the momentum. What investors can do when we band together is powerful.

In his book *To Change the World*, University of Virginia sociologist James Davison Hunter argues that we've underplayed the role and influence small numbers of people engaged at institutional levels have had on societal change. The cause of abolition can be traced to a few instrumental people like Charles Finney, who denied communion to slaveholders, and William Wilberforce, who catalyzed a small community intent on ending slavery. Greenpeace was a small group on the fringes thirty years ago, but today almost every Fortune 500 company makes a point to try to explain how they are environmentally compliant. World Vision is one nonprofit that began the whole idea of child sponsorship, and now billions of dollars flow into the underserved communities supporting children.

There's a whole other side to this to consider though. Even if we are having a small impact on a company, that company is still having a big impact on us. If I invest my dollars into a $200 billion market cap company, then sure, my little investment considered by itself (which, again, we shouldn't do) means little to the company. But I'm still getting dividends from that company and still counting on the share price increasing so that they will put profit in my pocket. Even if my investment is not meaningful to the company, the company is certainly meaningful to me. What is the company's impact on us and on our integrity?

Cassie Laymon, a financial advisor and friend, likes to say, "Whether or not your investment changes the wider world, I can tell you for sure that it will change your world." When we live faithful to our convictions and our hopes, this congruence does something deep inside us. When we know that we are consistently living out the things that we hold dear, we experience the joy of fulfilled purpose and a profound sense of ourselves and of the life we are living. What's more valuable to us than this?

If I'm buying stocks on the secondary market, or in a mutual fund or ETF, my money isn't going to that company but to other people who are selling those stocks. If I buy a used Honda Accord, my money doesn't go to Honda but instead to the prior owner of the Accord. Doesn't that mean I'm not actually supporting the company by my investing?

It's important to remember that regardless of how we acquire our shares, once we are a shareholder, we participate in and receive profit from whatever that company does. If we own shares, whether we think we're supporting the company or not, the company is supporting us. We are owners, and we benefit from that business.

Another way to think about it is this: If Larry starts a porn shop, and then I purchase it, my money goes into Larry's pocket rather than the porn company's. However, I now own the porn shop. I'm now responsible for that porn shop's products, just as Larry the founder was previously. The primary issue in investing is ownership, which is true no matter how or when we buy the shares.

Even aside from the ownership questions, our purchase of shares in a company on the secondary market still directly supports companies and the products they are producing in numerous ways. First, the stock market is a massive, interconnected enterprise. The secondary market requires the IPO market (where investors buy shares directly from the company) to create the mechanism undergirding the entire system. Without one, the other crumbles. If there was no secondary market, no company would ever be able to issue shares. The secondary market makes the primary market possible. In other words, if I wasn't willing to purchase Larry's porn shop for a high price, Larry might have never opened that shop in the first place.

Second, when a company's share price rises, it facilitates their ability to raise additional capital, either through issuing more shares or through private debt. When we invest in a company and help to raise its share price, we are helping the company secure a variety of kinds of funding.

Third, management teams are keenly sensitive to their company's share price. A company's board—as well as public perception—often looks at stock price performance as a primary indicator of whether the company is on the right track. Our purchases send a signal of support for the company's direction. Even more directly, shareholders are the ones who vote at shareholder meetings, providing governance over a company. As owners, we have influence (both active and passive) on a business.

Finally, secondary markets wield immense financial and social influence which shapes culture. Markets have enormous effect on global economies, public policies, and individual choices. The stock market is more than merely a dispassionate mechanism for buying and selling but a social force with immense impact over what we value, how we feel about our world, and how we view our civic responsibilities. When we invest in these markets, we participate in this entire infrastructure.

Are you using God and the Bible to peddle a product?

This has been one of Finny's and my concerns from the beginning. Our Christian understanding shapes our whole life, and so it must shape how we think about any business we would lead. That said, it's certainly true that there is a disturbing, grotesque marketing enterprise that uses Christian language and subculture to sell products. At Eventide, we want to lead with excellence and hope that people will be attracted to the quality of what we offer because they believe we articulate a better philosophy of investing. We hope that investors are drawn to Eventide because they see purpose and soundness in our investment philosophy and want to join us in seeking good investments and good returns.

The challenge for us is that we want to be able to share where our philosophy and vision come from, and the source is a comprehensive understanding of human flourishing emerging from Scripture and the teachings of Jesus. Our faith is not a sidenote but rather an illuminating light. For fellow Christians, we want to share why our hearts are inclined in this way—because we love God and want to live in ways that please God and serve our neighbors. For our friends and fellow investors who are not Christians, we want to find this common ground, based on a shared love for our neighborhoods and for a world of abundant goodness.

However, this whole conversation—this whole book— isn't ultimately about investing in Eventide. Our hope is for a sea change in the investing world that's so much bigger than Eventide and, if realized, would far outstrip our capacity. Our ultimate concern is not selling an investment product but rather seeing a world healed and renewed.

There's no such thing as a perfect company, and most every business in our imperfect world is probably tainted in some way. So, what difference does it really make which company I invest in?

Of course, it's true that there's no perfect company. Every company, like every human, is flawed. It's a misstep, though, to say that because perfection is impossible, I'm not responsible to make any qualitative assessments. We need to make judgments when clear evil or injustice is at work, and we should order our resources to encourage as much good as possible.

Imagine I put up two pictures side by side. One picture is of a child on the other side of the world holding a cigarette. The other picture is of a child with Duchenne muscular dystrophy, lying on her bed with her doctor by her side ready for a treatment that could restore some of her muscle deterioration. Both photos represent real investment opportunities. You can invest in a company that sells cigarettes to kids, or you can invest in a company that helps to heal children. Which one is better?

I love how my former colleague Sherrie Smith thinks through this. She explains how every company exists on a spectrum between practicing exploitation and promoting human flourishing and how our investments, even with imperfect companies, matter. Sherrie writes,

> As we push capital toward any given company on [this] continuum, we promote a world that looks more like the products and activities of that company. As we push capital toward companies providing waste services, we are pushing forward a cleaner, safer world. As we push capital toward companies in the solar energy space that are fighting for transparency in their own supply chains, we are advancing a world that is free of forced labor, where our own demand for energy doesn't come at the abuse of our global neighbors. As we push

capital toward companies leading in cybersecurity, we bring forward an online world that is safer for both our children and our aging loved ones. And as we push capital toward companies that are on the leading edge of Alzheimer's or cancer research, we are pursuing a world where the devastation of these diseases is eliminated.

I find it compelling to see that my goal as an investor is to push toward a world . . . defined by human flourishing, even while acknowledging that I may never see it fully achieved in my lifetime. I believe that we have each been given the resources we have for a reason. Why not use them for the greatest impact possible given our time and place in history?[106]

The fact is that we can make moral judgments, and, in fact, we do all the time. Lots of choices we make in everyday life require discernment and grappling with less-than-ideal realities. Most of us try to make wise choices for our health even though it's inevitable that in the end, we'll all die. Few of us ignore all political choices even though there's rarely any perfect, pristine clarity. We're always deciding what, given the options and current understanding, offers the *best* choice.

Scripture assumes that we must make judgments, instructing us to pursue righteousness and resist injustice. The choice may not always be clear, but sometimes it is. And even when it's not clear, we don't throw our hands in the air. Rather, we roll up our sleeves and do the hard work of making the best decision we can make. We have agency and the responsibility to live wisely.

This responsibility need not be a source of anxiety. We're not going to always get this right. I haven't always made the right choices. Maybe I didn't have the right information or maybe my judgement was flawed. Thankfully, we're only responsible to do our best, knowing that we're operating as an imperfect human in an imperfect world. But we *are* responsible to do our best.

Isn't it a matter of personal choice if I want to focus on making as much money as possible so that I can give more money away rather than thinking so much about the investment choices themselves?

Fundamentally, the answer for me is that the ends don't justify the means. We can't do good in the world if we're hurting the world in the process.

Peter Buffett, the son of probably the world's most influential investor Warren Buffett, wrote an opinion piece in the *New York Times* describing what he called "The Charitable-Industrial Complex."[107] Peter oversees a large philanthropic foundation tasked with giving away profits that his dad has made investing. One of the things Peter realized is that in many cases, he's trying to give money away to solve problems that are being created by ill-advised investors or short-sighted business practices. Some problems can't be fixed by charity, especially if the money funding that charity flows from the very activities creating the problem.

Philanthropy is wonderful. Buffett's own example of pledging to give away most of his wealth is exemplary. As of June 23, 2023, *USA Today* reported that Buffett had already donated $51.5 billion with far more to come.[108] This immense generosity has the capacity to do unmeasurable good in the world. However, our generosity must always also consider what good we're doing—or what problems we're creating—through the work we are pursuing in making our money to begin with.

We're called to bless the world and foster joy through every dimension of our lives. Our investments themselves can inflict damage or catalyze blessing. We're aiming to foster joy and nurture goodness with our investments, and then we want to do even *more* good by being generous with the profits that we've earned.

Do we have to stop shopping or working at companies that we wouldn't invest in? And if we don't, isn't that hypocritical?

I get this question pretty often. Financial advisors regularly ask me if I shop at companies that I wouldn't invest in, and the answer is yes. One person emailed our offices once to ask what kind of car Finny drove. The writer intended this as a gotcha question.

The fact is that I believe there is far more responsibility in ownership than in patronage. If I go to a convenience store and walk down the aisles, there will be pornography, tobacco, and lottery tickets on the shelves, sitting next to beef jerky, orange juice, and gum. When I walk out of the store carrying the gallon of milk I've purchased, I do so without any qualms. My choice to purchase milk means I'm a patron of milk, and my patronage encourages the business owner to put more milk on the shelf. Conversely, by not buying cigarettes or lottery tickets, I'm in a small way discouraging them from selling those products.

However, if I'm an investor in the convenience store, then I'm a part-owner who's profiting from the tobacco and everything else they sell. Of course, being an owner also means that I'd have more influence on the store to persuade them to stop selling cigarettes. The bottom line is that an owner/investor has a greater ethical/moral responsibility than the customer.

As for working for a company, we certainly should consider whether our work honors God and helps the world to flourish. Is our work good? Still, I think that employment is more akin to patronage than ownership. A person who works at a hotel cleaning the rooms has a very different role (hospitality) than someone responsible for arranging the partnerships to stream pornographic movies for customers. Cleaning rooms is good work that cares for others and creates beauty. Facilitating X-rated entertainment is exploitative work that harms others and mars beauty.

With all these things, we must always be gracious toward people who have few choices and are merely trying to keep their lives afloat. We should seek to create more meaningful work and better opportunities for everyone. Investors, however, have a lot of choices about where they will put their money.

ACKNOWLEDGMENTS

Writing is always a collective effort, gathering strands of thought and shards of influence, that are carefully crafted to make a mosaic we call a book. In these pages, this collective effort is especially true. My name is on the cover and my story is woven throughout, but this work carries the imprint of so many others.

I'm profoundly grateful for those who joined this effort because if they hadn't, this book would never have seen the light of day. Winn Collier helped to shape and write this entire work. Winn and I spent a lot of time together, and he even traveled with me to the small village in India where I grew up. Still, I am so impressed and overwhelmed by how Winn understood and expressed my heart and my story.

My beautiful and precious wife, Jaunita, and I were married the same year that Eventide was founded, and she has been my close advisor and supporter throughout this journey. I am so grateful to her because she has given me the ability to pursue my passion and has helped me every step of the way, while also managing our household affairs. God has blessed us with four beautiful children (Olivia, Christian, Gianna, and Ashton), and they bring us so much joy.

I am extremely grateful to Finny Kuruvilla. I have learned so much from him. There are many other jobs he could have taken out of grad school, but his commitment and vision to seeing investors align their investments with their values are unmatched. His leadership in this vision has brought excellence every day to our work. He is more than a partner; he is like an older brother and mentor to me. I would also like to thank Finny's parents, George and Leela Chavanikamannil, who have been such an encouragement and support to me.

Jason Myhre is the other founding member of Eventide to whom I am extremely grateful. While he officially joined Eventide at the end of 2009, he had already been a close friend who helped shape my thinking while we were founding Eventide. I am regularly encouraged by Jason's commitment to understanding and teaching God's heart and purposes for work and investing.

I am so thankful to work alongside and learn from Dolores Bamford on a daily basis. After serving as a Managing Director at Goldman Sachs and completing a seminary degree, Dolores joined Eventide because of her passion for our mission and values. Dolores told me once, "Eventide is the culmination of my faith, work, and life's mission."

Thank you Dolores for your constant encouragement and support.

I am so thankful for the leadership and support that both Carly Shotmeyer and Julie Jarrett provided in producing this book. Both Carly and Julie oversaw the crafting and editing of the story, and identifying writers, publishers, and marketers. Without their encouragement and close support, I am not sure that I would have had the endurance to finish this book.

There are also so many wonderful current and former colleagues I have gotten to work with every day in pursuing Eventide's wonderful mission together. Working with people who have such a high passion for our shared vision for the world provides me with so much energy for my work. Thank you for your passion and energy for this work. This is hard for me, but I am choosing not to name individuals because there are so many wonderful people I get to work alongside everyday in pursuing our mission. From the bottom of my heart, thank you for your commitment to our shared vision for the world, the excellence that you strive towards each and everyday in serving our clients, and for the love that you show one another every day.

One of the greatest blessings of my life has been to co-found and support Darsha Academy. Tom and Leena Varghese took on the momentous task of not only joining Jaunita and me in founding Darsha, but moving to

Bangalore India to oversee the school. I am so encouraged by the work the Lord has already done in these young women's lives, and am expectant for what is to come. Thank you, Tom and Leena, for the wonderful work you do each day to inspire and equip these students.

I am thankful for Ron Blue, Rob West, Sharon Epps, and the entire Kingdom Advisors organization for the wonderful work you do in helping Christian financial advisors integrate a biblical worldview into financial advice. I have attended all the annual conferences since 2009 and am amazed by how God has been moving within the community over the years. I am also so grateful that the Kingdom Advisors leadership has allowed the Eventide team to bring biblical thought leadership to the Kingdom Advisors community.

The work of the Faith and Work movement in the US has formed me, and I have been joined by so many team members who desire to align faith with our daily calling in the business marketplace. Thank you to Blake Schwarz of Central Commons who taught numerous classes to our team and has been a regular conversation partner to me. Jeff Haanen, Ross Chapman, and the team at Denver Institute for Faith and Work for your friendship and leadership in advancing this formation. Thank you to Julie Silander and the Charlotte Institute for Faith and Work for your thought leadership and cultivation of community. Thank you to Tom Nelson, Matt Rusten, and the Made to

Flourish team for your commitment to teaching pastors to share about the high calling of work from the pulpit. I'm grateful for the opportunity to spend the last several years with Dave Blanchard, Andy Crouch, Sajan George, and the Praxis team and have had the opportunity to witness the innovation and excellence they are bringing to redemptive capital and entrepreneurship.

Given that this is a book about good investing, it seems most fitting to thank the earliest investors that either provided us with capital to help get Eventide started or jumped in as an early consumer. Thank you Greg and JoAnn Gunter, Bill and Sallie Childers, Sony and Preeti Cheriakalath, Anil and Annie Thomas, Alan Seigel, Keith Boger, James Sanders, Roy Nunn, Jim Miller, Carter LeCraw, Alex Ellis, and John Wierenga. To Rick Laymon and Beacon Wealth Consultants: thank you for being the first advisor and firm to partner with us back in 2009. Your advocacy, support, and friendship over the years are invaluable. Finally, I would be remiss if I did not also thank Rusty Leonard of Stewardship Partners and Art Ally of Timothy Plan, the early pioneers of the biblically responsible investing movement; your efforts paved the path for our work and success. Thank you.

Finally, I want to thank my parents, John and Rajamma, my brother Sony Cheriakalath, my sister Julie Mathew, and the rest of my family for supporting me, especially with prayer, throughout my life.

NOTES

1. Jürgen Moltmann, *Joy and Human Flourishing: Essays on Theology, Culture, and the Good Life*, edited by Miroslav Volf (Fortress Press, 2015), 125.
2. Alfred, Lord Tennyson, *Ulysses* (1842).
3. Viktor E. Frankl, *Man's Search for Meaning* (Boston: Beacon Press, 2006), 40.
4. This became BNY Mellon in 2007 when Bank of New York merged with the Mellon Financial Corporation.
5. Katherine Boo, *Behind the Beautiful Forevers: Life, Death, and Hope in a Mumbai Undercity* (New York: Random House, 2012), xii.
6. Mary Clark Moschella, *Joy and Human Flourishing: Essays on Theology, Culture, and the Good Life*, edited by Miroslav Volf and Justin E. Crisp (Minneapolis: Fortress Press, 2015), 125.
7. Michelle Singletary, "More Americans Own Stocks. This Is Great for Their Financial Future," *The Washington Post*, accessed February 15, 2025, https://www.washingtonpost.com/business/2023/06/06/american-stock-ownership/.

8. "Monday—the Aidan Compline," *Celtic Daily Prayers*, accessed February 15, 2025, https://www.northumbria community.org/offices/monday-the-aidan-compline/.

9. Genesis 2:5–8 (NIV).

10. John H. Walton, *The New Application Commentary: Genesis* (Grand Rapids: Zondervan, 2001), 186. Old Testament scholar John Walton makes this point: "If people were going to fill the earth, we must conclude that they were not intended to stay in the garden in a static situation. Yet moving out of the garden would appear a hardship since the land outside the garden was not as hospitable as that inside the garden (otherwise the garden would not be distinguishable). Perhaps, then, we should surmise that people were gradually supposed to extend the garden as they went about subduing and ruling. Extending the garden would extend the food supply as well as extend sacred space (since that is what the garden represented)."

11. Dorothy Sayers, "Why Work?" https://www1.villanova.edu/content/dam/villanova/mission/faith/Why%20Work%20by%20Dorothy%20Sayers.pdf.

12. Ibid.

13. Jaqueline DeMarco, "55% of Americans Think Investing Is as Risky as Gambling," *Magnify Money*, October 1, 2019, https://www.magnifymoney.com/news/investing-as-risky-as-gambling-survey/.

14. Ellen Chang, "Buffet Blasts Wall Street as a Casino; Munger Attacks Robinhood," *The Street*, April 30, 2022. https://www.thestreet.com/investing/buffett-blasts-wall-street-as-a-casino-munger-attacks-robinhood.

15. Harry Pearson, interview by Tim Weinhold, Eventide Center for Faith & Investing, July 6, 2022, https://www.faithandinvesting.com/journal/an-advisors-journey-to-faithful-investing-with-harry-pearson/.

16. "Addressing Poverty with Redevelopment: Solutions to the Inequality Crisis in Dallas," *Communities United for a Greater Dallas*, www.datocms-assets.com/64990/1657040627-dallas-inequality-final.pdf.

17. Robert Wilsonky, "City Hall Offered $3M to Open a Grocery Store in a Southern Dallas Food Desert and Got No Takers," *Dallas Morning News*, November 30, 2016, https://www.dallasnews.com/news/politics/2016/11/30/city-hall-offered-3m-to-open-a-grocery-store-in-a-southern-dallas-food-desert-and-got-no-takers/ retrieved 1/2/24.

18. Brian Merchant, "Life and Death in Apple's Forbidden City," *The Guardian*, January 18, 2017, https://www.theguardian.com/technology/2017/jun/18/foxconn-life-death-forbidden-city-longhua-suicide-apple-iphone-brian-merchant-one-device-extract.

19. Fred Reichheld, *The Ultimate Question 2.0: How Net Promoter Companies Thrive in a Customer-Driven World* (Harvard Business Review Press, 2011).

20. Mihaly Csikszentmihalyi, *Good Business: Leadership, Flow, and the Making of Meaning* (Viking Adult, 2003). 25.

21. Malachi 3:5 (NET).

22. Isaiah 58:3 (NIV).

23. James 5:4 (MSG).

24. Robert Alter, *The Five Books of Moses: A Translation with Commentary* (W.W. Norton & Company, 2008). Every

productive possibility, every breath of life, every molecule of substance, requires God as its source in order to exist—and requires God for it to be sustained. However, God apparently intended for us to receive this bourgeoning life from Him and then join His unfolding venture, carrying His creative, world-shaping energy into the whole of creation. Genesis' opening sentence even hints at this, emphasizing how God initiates rather than completing creation. Hebrew scholar Robert Alter's revered translation reads, "When God *began to create* heaven and earth."

25. Proverbs 1:13 (NIV).
26. Tish Harrison Warren, "Why I'm Giving to This Environmental Group," *New York Times*, December 18, 2022, https://messaging-custom-newsletters.nytimes.com/dynamic/render?productCode=THW&uri=nyt%3A%2F%2Fnewsletter%2F47835ece-d8a5-5400-9473-76584c9ffbc0.
27. Warren, "Why I'm Giving."
28. Isaiah 65:17 (NIV).
29. Warren, "Why I'm Giving."
30. Luke 10:27 (ESV).
31. Galatians 5:14 (NIV).
32. This dialogue was adapted from Luke 10:30–37 (MSG).
33. These lines have often been attributed to Teresa of Ávila. However, it's possible the lines, though reflective of her thinking, have an uncertain origin. https://www.ncronline.org/spirituality/soul-seeing/soul-seeing/christ-has-no-body-earth-yours.
34. Milton Friedman, "A Friedman Doctrine—The Social Responsibility of Business Is to Increase Its Profits," *New York Times*, September 13, 1970, https://www.nytimes

.com/1970/09/13/archives/a-friedman-doctrine-the-social
-responsibility-of-business-is-to.html.

35. Fred Reichheld, *The Ultimate Question* (Cambridge, MA: Harvard Business School Press, 2006), 175.

36. Danny Klein, "McDonald's Settles Wage Theft Suite for $26 Million," *QSR,* November 25, 2019, https://www.qsr-magazine.com/fast-food/mcdonalds-settles-wage-theft-suit-26-million#:~:text=McDonald's%20settled%20a%20multi%2Dyear,corporate%20stores%20across%20the%20state.

37. Kevin and Jackie Freiberg, "20 Reasons Why Herb Kelleher Was One of the Most Beloved Leaders of Our Time," *Forbes,* updated April 7, 2019, https://www.forbes.com/sites/kevinandjackiefreiberg/2019/01/04/20-reasons-why-herb-kelleher-was-one-of-the-most-beloved-leaders-of-our-time/?sh=46b51e46b311.

38. There are a couple of versions of these lines from Kelleher, but I've pieced this together. Here are two versions: https://www.johnmillen.com/blog/leadership-lessons-ofsouthwest-airlines-ceo-herb-kelleher and https://www.forbes.com/sites/kevinandjackiefreiberg/2019/01/04/20-reasons-why-herb-kelleher-was-one-of-the-most-beloved-leaders-of-our-time/?sh=46b51e46b311.

39. R. Edward Freeman, interviewed by Business Roundtable Institute for Corporate Ethics, "Stakeholder Theory: Stakeholders are People," YouTube video, 2:08, October 1, 2009, https://www.youtube.com/watch?time_continue=106&v=keED9l3zVi8. Freeman is a professor of business administration at the University of Virginia Darden School of Business and the creator of stakeholder management theory.

40. This list was researched and compiled by the Great Place to Work Institute. I found that the top one hundred best companies to work for in America delivered stock returns that beat their peers by an average of 2.3 to 3.8 percent *per year* over a 28-year period. That's 89 percent to 184 percent cumulative.

41. Rob Schmitz, "What Hamburg's Missteps in 1892 Cholera Outbreak Can Teach Us About Covid-19 Response," *NPR*, May 6, 2020, https://www.npr.org/2020/05/06/849996451 /what-hamburgs-missteps-in-1892-cholera-outbreak-can -teach-us-about-covid-19-resp.

42. English physicist John Snow discovered the underlying mechanism of cholera in 1854 but could not identify the culprit. That same year, during an outbreak in Florence, Italian physician Filippo Pacini isolated the bacteria causing cholera, but Pacini's discovery was not widely noted. Thirty years later, Koch independently arrived at the same discovery and is widely credited with discovering the disease.

43. J. R. R. Tolkien, *The Hobbit* (Houghton Mifflin Harcourt, 2012), 199.

44. Jack Caporal, "How Many Americans Own Stock? About 162 Million—but the Wealthiest 1% Own More Than Half," *The Motley Fool*, December 27, 2024, https://www.fool .com/research/how-many-americans-own-stock/#:~:text =According%20to%20Gallup%2C%20162%20million,to %20access%20available%20viewer%20actions.

45. "The Tobacco Report: How Divesting from Tobacco Affected Returns over 20 Years," *Genus Fossil Free Investing*, February 2019, https://tobaccofreeportfolios.org/wp-con- tent/uploads/2020/05/Genus-Report.pdf.

46. Emily Dugan, "The Unstoppable March of the Tobacco Giants," *The Independent*, May 29, 2011, https://www .independent.co.uk/life-style/health-and-families/health -news/the-unstoppable-march-of-the-tobacco-giants -2290583.html.

47. As of September 30, 2024, data per Morningstar from December 2008 through October 2024.

48. Per Yahoo! Finance as of September 30, 2024.

49. World Health Organization, "Country Profile: Papua New Guinea," 2021, https://cdn.who.int/media/docs/default -source/country-profiles/tobacco/who_rgte_2021_papua _new_guinea.pdf?sfvrsn=c56defe8_5&download=true.

50. World Health Organization, *WHO Global Report on Trends in Prevalence of Tobacco Use 2000–2025*, 3rd ed., 2019, https://cdn.who.int/media/docs/default-source/searo/tobacco /country-fact-sheets/indonesia-who-tobacco-prevalence -trend-estimates-2019.pdf?sfvrsn=7391e26a_2.

51. Olivia Rondonuwu and Matthew Bigg, "Child Addicts at Heart of Indonesia Anti-Smoking Suit," *Reuters*, May 24, 2012, https://www.reuters.com/article/us-indonesia -smoking/child-addicts-at-heart-of-indonesia-anti-smoking -suit-idUSBRE84N0DF20120524.

52. Tim Weinhold, "The Smoking Gun of Mutual Funds," *Eventide Faith and Business* (blog), August 21, 2015, Eventide -Blog-15-8-21-The-Smoking-Gun-of-Mutual-Funds-1.pdf.

53. Morningstar data, accessed April 22, 2024. Top five holdings include tobacco company exposure for fourteen of fifteen years from 2009 to 2023.

54. Morningstar data, as of December 20, 2024.

55. "MO Major Holders," *Yahoo Finance*, accessed December 18, 2024, https://finance.yahoo.com/quote/MO/holders/; "PM Major Holders," *Yahoo Finance*, accessed December 18, 2024, https://finance.yahoo.com/quote/PM/holders/.

56. Romans 12:9 (NIV).

57. Isaiah 3:14 (NIV).

58. Isaiah 3:15 (NIV).

59. Deuteronomy 23:18 (NIV).

60. Proverbs 1:10–19 (ESV). I have played with the paraphrase to apply the Proverb to investors.

61. Romans 12:9 (NIV).

62. Matthew 27:6–10 (NIV).

63. Henry David Thoreau, *Walden, or, Life in the Woods* (1854), 57.

64. Harry Robertson, "Bill Hwang Lost Around $20 Billion in 2 Days when His Archegos Fund Imploded, Report Says," *Markets Insider*, April 9, 2021, https://markets.businessinsider.com/news/stocks/bill-hwang-lost-20-billion-2-days-archegos-collapse-report-2021-4-1030288757.

65. "Bill Hwang on Trial," *Financial Times*, May 8, 2024, https://www.ft.com/content/2f448cba-a9ac-4333-94f5-7200e20857f5.

66. ProPublica, "The Grace and Mercy Foundation Inc.," https://projects.propublica.org/nonprofits/organizations/208050779; Emily Belz, "Lawsuit Alleges Billionaire's Christian Foundation Engaged in Self-Dealing," *Christianity Today*, July 7, 2022, https://www.christianitytoday.com/news/2022/july/archegos-bill-hwang-grace-mercy-foundation-lawsuit.html.

67. Erik Schatzker, Sridhar Natarajan, and Katherine Burton, "Bill Hwang Had $20 Billion, Then Lost It All in Two Days," *Bloomberg*, April 8, 2021, https://www.bloomberg.com/news/features/2021-04-08/how-bill-hwang-of-archegos-capital-lost-20-billion-in-two-days.

68. Erik Schatzker, Sridhar Natarajan, and Katherine Burton, "Bill Hwang Had $20 Billion, Then Lost It All in Two Days," *Bloomberg Businessweek*, April 8, 2021, https://www.bloomberg.com/news/features/2021-04-08/how-bill-hwang-of-archegos-capital-lost-20-billion-in-two-days.

69. Schatzker, Natarajan, and Burton, "Bill Hwang Had $20 Billion."

70. Schatzker, Natarajan, and Burton, "Bill Hwang Had $20 Billion."

71. Paraphrased from "The Use of Money" by John Wesley (1744), https://www.preachingtoday.com/sermons/sermons/2010/july/useofmoney.html. There are many other pieces of wisdom in Wesley's sermon, all timely and worthy of our consideration.

72. Aveek Bhattacharya, Colin Angus, Robert Pryce, John Holmes, Alan Brennan, and Petra S. Meier, "How Dependent Is the Alcohol Industry on Heavy Drinking in England," National Library of Medicine, August 22, 2018, https://pubmed.ncbi.nlm.nih.gov/30136436/#:~:text=Findings%3A%20Those%20drinking%20above%20guideline,50%25%20of%20spirits%20sales%20value.

73. John Elflein, "Key Fact on Alcohol-Related Death Globally 2022," National Library of Medicine, May 22, 2024, https://www.statista.com/statistics/367890/alcohol-related-deaths-facts-worldwide/#:~:text=It%20is%20estimated

%20that%20alcohol,%2C%20cancer%2C%20and %20car%20accidents.

74. Adele Simmons, "Outside Opinion: Skeptics Were Wrong; South Africa Divestment Worked," *Chicago Tribune*, August 24, 2021, https://www.chicagotribune.com/2013 /12/15/outside-opinion-skeptics-were-wrong-south-africa -divestment-worked/.

75. Rob Moll, "Biblically Responsible Investing: Putting Our Money Where Our Values Are," *Christian News & Research*, April 25, 2007, https://www.epm.org/static/uploads/downloads /book-resources/Biblically_responsible_investing.pdf.

76. Matthew Hill, David Campanale, and Joel Gunter, "'Their Goal Is to Destroy Everyone': Uighur Camp Detainees Allege Systematic Rape," *BBC*, February 2, 2021, https:// www.bbc.com/news/world-asia-china-55794071.

77. Chris Buckley and Paul Mozur, "How China Uses High-Tech Surveillance to Subdue Minorities," *The New York Times*, May 22, 2019, https://www.nytimes.com/2019/05 /22/world/asia/china-surveillance-xinjiang.html.

78. Rebecca Wright, Ivan Watson, Zahid Mahmood and Tom Booth, "'Some Are Just Psychopaths': Chinese Detective in Exile Reveals Extent of Torture Against Uyghers," *CNN*, October 5, 2021, https://www.cnn.com/2021/10/04/china /xinjiang-detective-torture-intl-hnk-dst/index.html.

79. "Where Are Solar Panels Made?" Payaca, June 24, 2024, https://payaca.com/post/where-are-solar-panels-made.

80. Laura T. Murphy and Nyrola Elimä, "In Broad Daylight: Uyghur Forced Labour and Global Solar Supply Chains," produced through the Helena Kennedy Centre for International Justice at Sheffield Hallam University, https://www

.shu.ac.uk/helena-kennedy-centre-international-justice /research-and-projects/all-projects/in-broad-daylight.

81. Julie Tanner, "Investors Have Real Power to End Human Trafficking," *Institutional Investor*, September 5, 2016, https:// www.institutionalinvestor.com/article/b14z9n3jh2k1kw /investors-have-real-power-to-end-human-trafficking.

82. Gertrude Jekyll, *Wood and Garden: Notes and Thoughts, Practical and Critical, of a Working Amateur*, second edition (Longmans, Green, and Co., 1899), https://www.gutenberg .org/files/36279/36279-h/36279-h.htm.

83. Romans 12:9 (NIV).

84. Estelle Brachlianoff, "'A Business That Makes Nothing but Money Is a Poor Business' Henry Ford," *Huffington Post*, July 14, 2017, https://www.huffingtonpost.co.uk/estelle -brachlianoff/a-business-that-makes-not_b_10958310 .html.

85. Dave Roos, "7 Ways the Printing Press Changed the World," *History*, August 28, 2019, https://www.history.com /news/printing-press-renaissance.

86. Justin Champion, "'The Gutenberg Bible' Göttingen Library Edition review," *History Today* 68, no. 10 (2018), https:// www.historytoday.com/reviews/gutenberg%E2%80%99s -bible-real-information-revolution#:~:text=While%20the %20Gutenberg%20Bible%20was,opportunity%20and %20a%20cultural%20revolution.

87. "The Power of Investing: Promoting the Common Good," *Eventide*, https://www.eventideinvestments.com/wp-content /uploads/2021/07/Eventide-Whitepaper-Power-of-Investing -1.pdf. Much of this information is available in Eventide's white paper.

88. Katrin Flatscher, "Five Critical Reasons Rare Diseases Deserve Research Attention Now," *Tecan* (blog), https://www.tecan.com/blog/five-reasons-rare-diseases-deserve-research-attention-now.

89. World Health Organization, "Schizophrenia," January 10, 2022, https://www.who.int/news-room/fact-sheets/detail/schizophrenia; National Library of Medicine, "Employment Among People with Schizophrenia or Bipolar Disorder: A Population-Based Study Using Nationwide Registers," November 24, 2020, https://pmc.ncbi.nlm.nih.gov/articles/PMC7839734/; National Library of Medicine, "The Paradox of Premature Mortality in Schizophrenia: New Research Questions," November 24, 2010, https://pmc.ncbi.nlm.nih.gov/articles/PMC2951588/.

90. Katie Kingwell, "FDA Approves First Schizophrenia Drug with New Mechanism of Action Since 1950s," *Nature*, October 2, 2024, https://www.nature.com/articles/d41573-024-00155-8.

91. "New Study Offers Hope for Homeless People with Schizophrenia," *National Alliance to End Homelessness* (blog), December 3, 2015, https://endhomelessness.org/blog/new-study-offers-hope-for-homeless-people-with-schizophrenia/#:~:text=Schizophrenia%20affects%20a%20little%20more,and%20experiencing%20homelessness%20each%20day.

92. Ray Allegrezza, "How the Trucking Industry Stalled, and How It Can Be Fixed," *Business of Home*, January 4, 2022, https://businessofhome.com/articles/how-the-trucking-industry-stalled-and-how-it-can-be-fixed#:~:text=There%20has%20been%20a%20shortage,an%20already%20broken%20supply%20chain.

93. "Global Road Safety," CDC website, May 16, 2024, https://www.cdc.gov/transportation-safety/global/?CDC _AAref_Val=https://www.cdc.gov/injury/features/global -road-safety/index.html.

94. "The Business 360 Framework," *Eventide,* https://www .eventideinvestments.com/business-360/.

95. Winn Collier, "Resurrection & Creation," April 25, 2022, https://winncollier.com/the-resurrection-creation/.

96. Annie Dillard, *The Writing Life* (Harper Perennial: 1990), 78.

97. Deut. 24:15; Mal. 3:5.

98. This is not an exhaustive list of our investments, and allocations are subject to change.

99. Thank you to Adrian Merryman at VisionFund for helping to research and collect these stories.

100. "Frugal Woman Dies at 100, Donates $35.6M," *NBC News,* October 18, 2006, https://www.nbcnews.com/id /wbna15315697; "A Magnificent Gift for Cure-Focused Research," http://newsletter.miami.edu/med-archives/web /scrip/january2007/story04.html; "Former Beautician Leaves $35.6 Million for Cancer and Diabetes Research," *Candid,* October 21, 2006, https://philanthropynewsdigest .org/news/former-beautician-leaves-35.6-million-for-cancer -and-diabetes-research.

101. Giovanni Marassutti, interview by Edward Sylvan, *Authority Magazine,* April 5, 2021, https://medium.com /authority-magazine/stars-making-a-social-impact-why -how-actor-giovanni-morassutti-is-helping-to-change-our -world-8684d8964338. Past performance is no guarantee of future returns.

102. Tyler Wigg Stevenson, "A Merciful White Flash," *Christianity Today*, April, 2008, https://www.christianitytoday.com/ct/2008/april/nuclear-war-merciful-white-flash.html.

103. "S&P 500 Environmental & Socially Responsible Index," *S&P Global, Inc.*, https://www.spglobal.com/spdji/en/indices/sustainability/sp-500-environmental-socially-responsible-index/#overview; "S&P 500," *S&P Global, Inc.*, https://www.spglobal.com/spdji/en/indices/equity/sp-500/#overview. Comparing the ten year returns of the S&P 500 Environmental and Socially Responsible Index (11.49 % annual return) with the standard S&P 500 Index (11.04 % annual return), as of December 19, 2024, via S&P Global. Past performance is no guarantee of future returns.

104. Jon Hale, "Sustainable Investing Research Suggests No Performance Penalty," *Morningstar, Inc.*, November 10, 2016, https://www.morningstar.com/sustainable-investing/sustainable-investing-research-suggests-no-performance-penalty.

105. Fred Reichheld, *The Ultimate Question* (Harvard Business School Press, 2006), 175.

106. Sherrie Johnson Smith, "Is There Any Perfect Company?" *Eventide*, January 30, 2023, https://www.eventideinvestments.com/insights/is-there-any-perfect-company/.

107. Peter Buffett, "The Charitable-Industrial Complex," *New York Times*, July 26, 2013, https://www.nytimes.com/2013/07/27/opinion/the-charitable-industrial-complex.html.

108. Jessica Guynn, "Buffett, World's Sixth Richest Man, Just Donated Billions More in Berkshire Hathaway Stock," *USA Today*, June 23, 2023, https://www.usatoday.com/story/money/2023/06/23/warren-buffett-donates-billions-berkshire-hathaway-stock/70352728007/.